Signs of a Great Bookshop

If you're doing the following, you're serving your customers' needs in spades:

- **You remember the faces, names, and favorite books of your customers.** Service is about building a long-term relationship, so study the faces of your customers.

- **You're constantly on the lookout for new customers.** Healthy bookstores don't remain static. They reach out to new customers and to new markets.

- **The atmosphere in your bookshop is comfortable, safe, and reflective of your individual community.** Be sure that your store is unique, drawing from your community to create an atmosphere that fits you and your customers.

- **Your store is well-stocked, and you pay your bills on time.** Everybody has the occasional cash-flow problem (see Chapter 13), but a vital bookstore produces more income than stress.

- **You and your staff are knowledgeable about books in general and the categories you carry in particular.** With this knowledge, you can place a book in a customer's hands and make a great match between book and booklover.

- **You help book clubs manage their selections.** Although your input may not be accepted, offer your help in getting book clubs started, in understanding how to generate healthy discussion, and in organization.

- **You fill special orders efficiently and quickly.** Place a special order the day it's requested, and the order may be delivered the next day. That thrills a customer.

- **You're accessible, either in person, by phone, or via e-mail.** Make yourself accessible, and you make customers loyal.

- **You offer dead-on, interesting events that customers can't wait to attend.** Events should add to the quality of your customers' lives and use their time wisely.

- **You provide well-chosen free services, such as gift wrapping, delivery, shipping, or gift registry.** Want to create a loyal customer in a snap? Offer these services and do them well.

- **Your business hours match your customers' needs.** Consider opening later one or two days a week and staying open later in the evening, too. Or, survey customers to find out what hours are most useful to them.

- **You have a Web site up and running or under construction.** You may not sell tons of books on the Web, but the site is a convenience that your customers appreciate and, increasingly, expect from you.

Bookselling For Dummies®

Cheat Sheet

Reviewing Glossary Terms

The following terms are ones every bookseller should know!

advance reading copy (ARC): Prepublication version of a book.

assets: Money you have ready, expect to receive, or can get from selling something you own.

backlist: Books across all categories that have been on the market for a while and are proven sellers.

break out: To produce stronger than expected sales.

cash-wrap: Area where customers pay for their purchases before leaving the store.

categories: Subject groupings of books; also known as *sections*.

co-op money: Money paid from publishers to booksellers to help promote their books; co-op money is tied to a bookseller's purchases from publishers.

cost: Amount your inventory cost you to buy.

destination categories: Popular categories that draw people to them.

display pack: Cardboard or other display that may sit on the floor or on a counter or table. Also known as a *counterpack, dump,* or *floor display*.

face out: Shelve a book so that its front cover shows, rather than its spine.

feature display: A display of key titles or special books, usually built on a table or other horizontal surface.

financial benchmarks: Numbers to which you can compare your store.

floor displays: Another name for display pack.

frontlist: New titles from publishers.

galley: Advance reading copy.

handsell: Personally recommending a book to a customer.

inventory turn: Each time a book sells.

keystoning: Doubling (or more) your cost to arrive at your retail price.

laydown date: The first date that booksellers can display a book.

list: Amount for which you sell books. Also known as *retail*.

loss leaders: Books or other products priced to break even or lose money with the intention of drawing customers to the store.

margins: The difference between what you pay for something and what you can sell it for.

midlist: Frontlist titles that are expected to produce modest sales. See also *frontlist*.

open-to-buy: Budgeted amount you can spend on inventory.

out-of-stock: Book that's not available when you place an order.

remainders: Publishers' overstocks sold to booksellers at greatly reduced prices.

sales velocity: Whether the title is gaining momentum, remaining static, or decreasing in sales.

short discount: Small discount.

sidelines: Non-book products that supplement book sales.

slat wall: Wood or laminate material with horizontal grooves or slats used to display products.

sleeper: Midlist title that exceeds publisher's expectations. See also *midlist*.

special order: A customer order you place for a book you don't have in stock.

visual merchandising: Describes the way you organize, display, and sell products.

wholesalers: Book middlemen who buy from publishers and sell to retailers. Also known as *distributors* or *jobbers*.

work the buy: Decide which frontlist titles to order. See also *frontlist*.

Copyright © 2003 Wiley Publishing, Inc. All rights reserved.

Item 4051-3.

For more information about Wiley Publishing, call 1-800-762-2974.

For Dummies: Bestselling Book Series for Beginners

Bookselling

FOR

DUMMIES®

by Tere Stouffer Drenth,

with contributions by independent booksellers nationwide

Kate Whouley, Technical Editor

Foreword by George Stanley, Vice President, Director of Sales,
Professional and Trade Division, and Rob Dyer, Director of Trade
Sales, Independent Accounts, John Wiley & Sons

WILEY

Wiley Publishing, Inc.

Bookselling For Dummies®

Published by
Wiley Publishing, Inc.
909 Third Avenue
New York, NY 10022
www.wiley.com

Copyright © 2003 by Wiley Publishing, Inc., Indianapolis, Indiana

Published by Wiley Publishing, Inc., Indianapolis, Indiana

Published simultaneously in Canada

No part of this publication may be reproduced, stored in a retrieval system, or transmitted in any form or by any means, electronic, mechanical, photocopying, recording, scanning, or otherwise, except as permitted under Sections 107 or 108 of the 1976 United States Copyright Act, without either the prior written permission of the Publisher, or authorization through payment of the appropriate per-copy fee to the Copyright Clearance Center, 222 Rosewood Drive, Danvers, MA 01923, 978-750-8400, fax 978-646-8700. Requests to the Publisher for permission should be addressed to the Legal Department, Wiley Publishing, Inc., 10475 Crosspoint Blvd., Indianapolis, IN 46256, 317-572-3447, fax 317-572-4447, or e-mail permcoordinator@wiley.com.

Trademarks: Wiley, the Wiley Publishing logo, For Dummies, the Dummies Man logo, A Reference for the Rest of Us!, The Dummies Way, Dummies Daily, The Fun and Easy Way, Dummies.com and related trade dress are trademarks or registered trademarks of Wiley Publishing, Inc., in the United States and other countries, and may not be used without written permission. All other trademarks are the property of their respective owners. Wiley Publishing, Inc., is not associated with any product or vendor mentioned in this book.

ISBN: 0-7645-4051-3

Manufactured in the United States of America

10 9 8 7 6 5 4 3 2 1

LIMIT OF LIABILITY/DISCLAIMER OF WARRANTY: WHILE THE PUBLISHER AND AUTHOR HAVE USED THEIR BEST EFFORTS IN PREPARING THIS BOOK, THEY MAKE NO REPRESENTATIONS OR WARRANTIES WITH RESPECT TO THE ACCURACY OR COMPLETENESS OF THE CONTENTS OF THIS BOOK AND SPECIFICALLY DISCLAIM ANY IMPLIED WARRANTIES OF MERCHANTABILITY OR FITNESS FOR A PARTICULAR PURPOSE. NO WARRANTY MAY BE CREATED OR EXTENDED BY SALES REPRESENTATIVES OR WRITTEN SALES MATERIALS. THE ADVICE AND STRATEGIES CONTAINED HEREIN MAY NOT BE SUITABLE FOR YOUR SITUATION. YOU SHOULD CONSULT WITH A PROFESSIONAL WHERE APPROPRIATE. NEITHER THE PUBLISHER NOR AUTHOR SHALL BE LIABLE FOR ANY LOSS OF PROFIT OR ANY OTHER COMMERCIAL DAMAGES, INCLUDING BUT NOT LIMITED TO SPECIAL, INCIDENTAL, CONSEQUENTIAL, OR OTHER DAMAGES.

For general information on our other products and services or to obtain technical support, please contact our Customer Care Department within the U.S. at 800-762-2974, outside the U.S. at 317-572-3993, or fax 317-572-4002.

Wiley also publishes its books in a variety of electronic formats. Some content that appears in print may not be available in electronic books.

WILEY is a trademark of Wiley Publishing, Inc.

About the Author

Tere Stouffer Drenth, a dyed-in-the-wool fan of independent bookshops, once dreamed of someday running her own children's bookstore. Interviewing booksellers from across the country, however, quickly made her realize the folly of that dream!

As a diversion from full-time freelance writing and editing, Tere also runs road races professionally — she is the author of the newly released *Marathon Training For Dummies* (Wiley Publishing, Inc.), as well as several other general reference books.

Tere (which rhymes with "Mary") lives in Charlevoix, Michigan, with her husband, Doug Drenth, and two rambunctious Labrador retrievers. You can reach her at tdrenth@earthlink.net.

About the Technical Editor

Kate Whouley (whoo-lee, rhymes with "truly") works with booksellers across the U.S. and abroad on a variety of projects, from designing new stores and store expansions to advising bookstore owners on operational and financial matters. An active contributor to book-industry publications, Kate is the Editor of *Manual on Bookselling,* 5th Edition. She is also Series Editor for ABA's *Fundamentals of Bookselling* and the author of "Customers and Service" in that series. Kate is presently at work on two books unrelated to bookselling: a nonfiction project, *Cottage for Sale: Must Be Moved* (slated for May 2004 publication from Commonwealth Editions), and a novel, *The Memory of Laughter.* She can be reached via her Web site at www.booksincommon.com.

Acknowledgments

Compiling this book was a fascinating challenge that involved more than 60 book-industry professionals, all of whom deserve a hearty "thank you." Thanks to **P.J. Campbell** (Director of Events) and **John Helmus** (Director of Trade Sales, Market Planning) at Wiley Publishing, Inc., who inspired this book and worked with ABA to bring it to life. Thanks, also, to **Dan Cullen,** Director of Information at ABA, who worked extensively with **Kate Whouley,** this book's amazing technical editor, who was always professional but also so much fun to work with. Other ABA and ABFFE staff who contributed their time and talents include **Carl Lennertz, Oren Teicher, Mark Nichols, Jill Perlstein, Chris Finan,** and **Kristen Gilligan.** More than 30 booksellers from around the country (see the "About the Contributors" page) lent their expertise to the project by participating in interviews. This book wouldn't have been possible without them, and I thank them for their time and patience.

Extra-special thanks to **Zoë Wykes,** Senior Project Editor, and **Stephanie Corby,** Brand Management Editorial Manager, who planned and managed every detail of the project, from coordinating deadlines to editing the manuscript to designing and reviewing the cover — and who also became friends along the way. **Jan Withers,** who coordinated page proofs and reviewed the final copy for errors, did a terrific job. And thanks to Wiley's Composition team, including **Karl Brandt, Amanda Carter, David Faust, LeAndra Johnson, Jay Kern, Janet Seib, Rob Springer, Julie Trippetti,** and **Erin Zeltner,** who managed to produce this book on the tightest deadline imaginable.

About the Contributors

Larry Abramoff owns Tatnuck Bookseller in Worcester, Massachusetts, where he specializes in fun and martinis. Larry contributed to Chapter 8.

Andrea Avantaggio and **Peter Schertz** co-own Maria's Bookshop (Durango, Colorado), a general bookstore specializing in books of the Southwest. Andrea and Peter contributed to Chapter 8.

Beverly Bittarelli manages Book Ends, a general bookstore in Winchester, Massachusetts. Beverly contributed her expertise on special orders to Chapter 9.

David Bolduc owns the Boulder Book Store, which takes up four floors of a historic building in downtown Boulder, Colorado. David contributed to Chapter 9.

Gilda Bruckman started New Words Bookstore in 1974 with three other women. Today, Gilda is planning to open the Center for New Words, a not-for-profit organization that encourages women and girls to write. Gilda contributed to Chapter 2.

Tom Campbell co-owns The Regulator Bookshop in Durham, North Carolina, which he took online (www.regbook.com) a few years ago. Tom contributed to Chapter 10.

Susan Capaldi manages McLean & Eakin Booksellers in beautiful Petoskey, Michigan. The ten-year-old store, owned by Julie Norcross, has tripled in size since it opened. Susan contributed to Chapter 11.

Dan Chartrand founded Water Street Bookstore (Exeter, New Hampshire) in 1991 with co-owner Robert Hugo. Dan contributed to Chapters 3 and 9.

Avin Mark Domnitz has been CEO of the American Booksellers Association since 1998. A graduate of the University of Wisconsin Law School, Avin entered bookselling in 1979. He was elected to the ABA board in 1988. Avin contributed to Chapter 13.

Wayne "Rusty" Drugan is the Executive Director of the New England Booksellers Association. He is a former bookseller with 15 years of experience. Rusty contributed to Chapters 1 and 8.

Carole Horne is head buyer and vice president of merchandising at Harvard Book Stores, Inc., in Cambridge, Massachusetts, where she has worked for 28 years. Carol contributed to Chapters 5 and 6.

Michael Hoynes is the marketing director with the American Booksellers Association, where he is heavily involved in the Book Sense and LMI programs. Michael contributed to Chapters 3 and 8.

Bob Hugo opened the Spirit of '76 Bookstore in Marblehead, Massachusetts, while still a student at the University of Massachusetts. Today, he owns three stores on Boston's north shore and co-owns two others in New Hampshire. Bob contributed to Chapters 14 and 15.

Vivien Jennings is founder and president of Rainy Day Books, Inc., in Fairway, Kansas (near Kansas City), which she opened in 1975 and co-operates with partner Roger Doeren. Vivien contributed to Chapters 3 and 9.

Mitchell Kaplan has been a bookseller for over 20 years, establishing Books & Books in 1982. Books & Books is a general, trade bookstore serving the South Florida community, with locations in Coral Gables and Miami Beach. Mitchell contributed to Chapters 7 and 8.

Sally and **George Kiskaddon** opened Builders Booksource in 1982, just a year after they married. Sally and George contributed to Chapters 4 and 9.

Michele Lewis owns the Afro-American Book Stop in New Orleans, Louisiana, a bookshop that offers books for and about African Americans. Michele contributed to Chapter 8.

Annette Meurer is the marketing and public relations manager for Joseph-Beth Booksellers in Cincinnati, Ohio, which has been in business for ten years. Annette contributed to Chapter 8.

Linda Mileman joined Tattered Cover Book Store in 1979, when the store employed just ten staff members. Today, Linda is one of two general managers (along with Matt Miller) who oversee 220 employees at Tattered Cover, which is owned by Joyce Meskis. Linda contributed to Chapter 11.

Barbara Morrow and **Ed Morrow** started Northshire Bookstore in Manchester, Vermont, in 1976 and moved to a new location, which they are now expanding, in 1985. Barbara and Ed contributed to Chapters 2, 5, and 6.

Karl Pohrt opened Shaman Drum in 1980, right around the corner form the flagship Borders store in Ann Arbor, Michigan. Karl contributed to Chapter 4.

Jake Reiss is the owner of The Alabama Booksmith in Birmingham, Alabama. Visit his Web site at www.alabama-booksmith.com. Jake contributed to Chapters 8 and 10.

Peter Schertz (*see* **Andrea Avantaggio** and **Peter Schertz**).

Alan Schmidt bought Book Etc in Portland, Maine, 15 years ago and opened a second store in Falmouth, Maine, in 2000. Alan contributed to Chapter 7.

Robert Segedy has been in the book business for over 16 years. Now an independent book reviewer, he resides in Pittsboro, North Carolina, with his wife, Jennifer, and two bad cats. Robert contributed to Chapters 5 and 6.

Gayle Shanks and **Bobby Sommer** co-own Changing Hands, a 10,000-square-foot bookstore in Tempe, Arizona, that offers new and used books and an astounding selection of sidelines. Gayle and Bobby contributed to Chapter 4.

Barbara Siepker purchased the name and inventory of The Cottage Book Shop seven years ago and moved it to a 1,000-square-foot log cabin in Glen Arbor, Michigan, in the heart of Sleeping Bear Dunes National Lakeshore. Barbara contributed to Chapter 11.

Neal Sofman, owner of A Clean Well-Lighted Place for Books in San Francisco, California, projects his cash flow every day. Neal contributed to Chapter 13.

Bobby Sommer (*see* **Gayle Shanks** and **Bobby Sommer**).

Sandy Torkildson owns A Room of One's Own Feminist Bookstore, a proud part of the feminist community in Madison, Wisconsin, for 27 years. Sandy contributed to Chapter 8.

Len Vlahos is the director of BookSense.com. Before joining ABA, Len worked for a variety of bookstores, including an independent and a university store. Len contributed to Chapter 10.

Publisher's Acknowledgments

We're proud of this book; please send us your comments through our Dummies online registration form located at www.dummies.com/register/.

Some of the people who helped bring this book to market include the following:

Acquisitions, Editorial, and Media Development

Senior Project Editor: Zoë Wykes

Editorial Manager: Stephanie Corby

Cartoons: Rich Tennant, www.the5thwave.com

Production

Project Coordinator: Jay Kern

Layout and Graphics: Karl Brandt, Amanda Carter, LeAndra Johnson, Julie Trippetti, Erin Zeltner

Proofreader: David Faust

Indexer: Sherry Massey

Special Help: P.J. Campbell, John Helmus, Jan Withers

Publishing and Editorial for Consumer Dummies

Diane Graves Steele, Vice President and Publisher, Consumer Dummies

Joyce Pepple, Acquisitions Director, Consumer Dummies

Kristin A. Cocks, Product Development Director, Consumer Dummies

Michael Spring, Vice President and Publisher, Travel

Brice Gosnell, Publishing Director, Travel

Suzanne Jannetta, Editorial Director, Travel

Publishing for Technology Dummies

Andy Cummings, Vice President and Publisher, Dummies Technology/General User

Composition Services

Gerry Fahey, Vice President of Production Services

Debbie Stailey, Director of Composition Services

Table of Contents

Chapter 17: Ten Reasons Why Bookselling Is the Best Job Ever 213

Foreword

● ●

*P*ublishing a book exclusively for our bookselling partners immediately impressed us as a good idea. After all, the bookselling environment is changing faster than at any other time in history, and as a result, community-based independent booksellers face both increased pressures and new opportunities. Whether you're looking to start a Web site, host more and better events, or manage your cash flow more efficiently, this book helps you compete in today's bookselling market.

Our intention in publishing *Bookselling For Dummies* is to offer ideas and insights about managing an independent bookstore and finding opportunities for additional sales and revenue generation. This book not only helps novice booksellers discover the basics of bookselling, but also shares tried and true techniques to inspire more experienced booksellers. If we're able to help improve your bottom line in *any* way, we will have accomplished what we set out to do.

Wiley is proud of the *For Dummies* line of books and its philosophy of approaching any topic in a fun and easy way. Each book is designed with a clean and open format, as well as crisp, concise, and clear writing. Referencing is easy, and the advice is straightforward, without talking down to the reader or presupposing any knowledge of publishing jargon. With over 100 million books in print, *For Dummies* is truly an international icon.

George Stanley
Vice President, Director of Sales, Professional and Trade Division
John Wiley & Sons, Inc.

Rob Dyer
Director of Trade Sales, Independent Accounts
John Wiley & Sons, Inc.

Introduction

● ●

*H*ere's a wild guess at what you're thinking right now: "I'm no bookselling dummy!" If that's what's in your head, you're absolutely right. No one at Wiley Publishing, Inc., thinks you're a dummy about anything — especially about bookselling. In fact, while compiling this book, two truths about booksellers emerged:

- ✔ Booksellers are ultra-smart.
- ✔ Most booksellers spend every day of their lives discovering more and more.

Whether you're fairly new to bookselling and are looking for a host of ideas, you've been in business for a long time and are looking to make a savvy change to better compete with other businesses, or you're running a super-successful bookstore and want to read this book for fun (and, perhaps, pick up one good tip in the process), *Bookselling For Dummies* is for you. With this book, you benefit from the experience and knowledge of your colleagues and mentors who run terrific independent bookshops around the country.

About This Book

Bookselling For Dummies is written for independent booksellers who are already in business, so the book skips over information that's not likely to be relevant to you, like choosing a location, leasing or buying property, laying out your store, buying your initial inventory, and taking out insurance. Rather, this book focuses on making your day-in, day-out operations more successful, from expanding into new categories and ordering frontlist titles to generating a buzz about your store, creating an online presence, managing employees, and handling paperwork. Every piece of information has been gleaned from independent booksellers across the country.

After you've digested everything you can from this book, pass it along to your manager(s), buyer(s), and other employees. Even though this book is written for you, your staff can likely pick up some tips from it, as well.

Conventions Used in This Book

Like all *For Dummies* books, this book avoids techno-jargon and other confusing terms that make you scratch your head in wonder. Instead, whenever a new term is used, the term is presented in italics, *like this,* and followed by a brief definition.

A few basic terms, however, are included without definitions, and they include the following:

- ✔ **American Booksellers Association (ABA):** The not-for-profit trade association of booksellers across the country. Booksellers join ABA, pay an annual fee, and receive a host of services in return.

- ✔ **Independent bookseller:** A privately owned and operated bookstore or small group of bookstores.

- ✔ **Internet-based booksellers and book clubs:** Booksellers that don't offer a physical storefront. All of their business is generated through Internet sales and catalog orders. Amazon.com is the most recognizable Internet-based bookseller; Quality Paperback Book Club (QPBC) is one of the largest book clubs in the world.

- ✔ **National bookstore chain stores (also called *corporate superstores*):** These bookstores are spread over a wide geographic area, but maintain a corporate office in one city, from which all (or nearly all) of the frontlist buying decisions are made. Most carry books, music, and videos and feature a full-service café. Barnes & Noble and Borders are the largest corporate chains in the United States.

- ✔ **Price clubs:** Price clubs charge an annual fee and give out membership cards. Customers can then enter a warehouse (with cinder-block walls and concrete floors) and purchase large quantities of products at substantial discounts. During the last decade, price clubs have begun carrying books — often remainders (see Chapter 4) but

also bestsellers and multi-volume sets of popular books —
at substantial discounts. Sam's Club and Costco are the
two most popular price clubs.

✔ **Mass merchandisers:** These stores — Wal-Mart, Target,
Meijer, for example — sell all sorts of household products and a large number of popular adult, children's, and
religious books. Books may be positioned as gifts and as
impulse buys for customers themselves. Mass merchandisers may be able to sway publishing decisions because
of their large volume. Office-supply superstores may also
fall into this category, because they may carry a large
selection of computer and business books.

Foolish Assumptions

Bookselling For Dummies makes only one foolish assumption
about you, dear reader: You own, manage, or otherwise work
in an independent bookshop.

How This Book Is Organized

To make your trip through a *For Dummies* book not only
enjoyable but also efficient, each book is separated into *parts*
that focus on a particular subject area. This book includes five
such parts, and they're organized as follows.

Part 1: The Joy of Bookselling

This part gives you an overview of the bookselling business,
starting with an introductory chapter that tells you where to
find bookselling buddies: the ABA, your regional bookselling
association, and so on.

This part also helps you with business planning, helping you
redefine your mission, vision, goals, objectives, strengths,
weaknesses, opportunities, and threats. You also get an entire
chapter that helps you find out why customers are (or aren't)
buying your products and figure out ways to intelligently
target certain products and services to customers who want
what you're offering.

Part II: Managing Your Product

This part gets you into the nitty-gritty of the bookselling business, including a chapter that discusses how to manage your existing categories and decide whether to carry additional categories. You also find great information about buying frontlist titles, sourcing used books, and tracking down sidelines. And mostly, you find tips and tricks for successfully managing your inventory.

Part III: Selling Books and Serving Your Customers

This part covers the gamut of selling books. You start off with a chapter that helps you establish your store's ambiance and move right into one of the meatiest chapters in the book: how to get customers in the door. You also get information on working your store into your community — from joining the Chamber of Commerce to hooking up with other merchants and not-for-profits in your area. You find out how to sell gently to your customers (but sell, nonetheless), assuring repeat business and looking for new sales opportunities.

In this part, you also find a special chapter that discusses ways that you can create — or improve — your online presence, thus serving your customers that much better.

Part IV: Running an Efficient Small Business

Your bookshop is a small business, so as much as you may want to focus on ordering, selling, and holding events about books, you also need to manage employees, pay taxes, and balance your books. This part gives you the lowdown.

Part V: The Part of Tens

The Part of Tens is a staple in every *For Dummies* book and is known far and wide for being fun, easy-to-read, and full of great ideas. In this part, you find ten ideas for attracting customers, ten ways to lower costs, ten terrific ideas for motivating employees, and ten reasons why bookselling is the best job in the world.

Icons Used in This Book

Icons are small pictures in the margins of this book that highlight the text in a special way. Think of icons as road signs that help you steer in the proper direction, around obstacles, and with all the information you need at your disposal. Here's a quick list of what the icons mean:

 Next to this icon, you find real-world examples from booksellers across the country. Not every example applies to your store or your geographic area, but each example illustrates a point vividly.

 This icon highlights book-industry terms that are defined for you. You won't have to spell them or use them in a sentence at BEA or your regional association trade show, but they'll make you sound like a bookselling guru if you sprinkle them into your everyday conversation.

 Think of these tidbits of information as information to tattoo on your brain — or if you're somewhat less adventurous, cut out and stick on your refrigerator — as constant reminders from bookselling experts.

 This icon presents you with tips, tricks, and techniques that make you a better bookseller and make your store more profitable.

 Danger, warning, sound the alarm bells! This icon helps you negotiate the difficult waters of bookselling without making a wrong move.

Where to Go from Here

The beauty of *For Dummies* books is that you don't have to read them from start to finish. Rather, you can pick up this book, open it to any page, and start reading. If you want to direct your reading a bit, check out the Table of Contents at the front of this book or the Index at the back and look for whatever topics interest you most.

Of course, if you want to read this book from cover to cover, you're welcome to do so. You'll pick up some great tips to better bookselling and have some fun along the way.

Part I
The Joy of Bookselling

The 5th Wave   By Rich Tennant

In this part . . .

You discover the many joys of bookselling — and a few of the downsides, too! This part introduces you to bookselling friends and resources you can tap for practical advice and tips. You also find out how to evaluate and position your store to meet today's demands and challenges and how to plan your business into the future. You look at your mission, vision of the future, goals and objectives, strengths and weaknesses, and opportunities and threats.

This part also helps you look deeply into the desires and intentions of your customers, finding out what motivates them to buy, why they sometimes choose not to, and in what ways you can better meet their needs. Finally, you get the lowdown on the ABA's Local Marketing Intelligence (LMI) program.

Chapter 1

Getting a Little Help from Your Bookselling Friends

*R*unning a bookstore is distinctly different from running any other type of retail store. If you're an independent bookseller, your job and your business is even more unique. You may be the only bookstore for miles around, which means you don't have any local bookselling colleagues with whom to share ideas, garner advice, or commiserate. This chapter helps you find your bookselling friends and get a little help, not the least of which comes from this friendly guide, which offers loads of practical advice and suggestions.

Joining the American Booksellers Association

Although you may not find bookselling buddies in your local town, you can find them nationally and regionally. The American Booksellers Association (ABA), for example, is a national community of booksellers that provides advocacy, offers opportunities for peer interaction (which means no more operating in isolation), offers educational opportunities, provides support to owners of bookstores, and introduces new business models to help you compete more effectively. The American Booksellers Association is governed by a nine-member Board of Directors, all of whom are active booksellers. Working in conjunction with the volunteer leadership is an advisory council of booksellers, plus a professional staff.

ABA holds its annual convention in conjunction with BookExpo America (BEA), arguably the most important book-related trade show in the world. ABA provides a great deal of educational programming at BEA, including workshops and panel discussions.

Among ABA's many great offerings is the Book Sense program (see Chapter 8), which links your store with other participating bookstores, raising the profile of independent booksellers nationwide. Book Sense encourages customers to visit your store through recommended books, national advertising and promotional material, and gift certificates. Through Book Sense, you can develop a BookSense.com Web site, which costs less than the price of a business-card-size ad in most newspapers and can often be fully paid for by co-op money (see Chapter 4).

Membership in ABA is on a sliding scale that's based on your store's annual book sales. ABA also offers provisional membership to individuals planning to open a bookstore and associate membership to others allied with the field. To find out how to join ABA, log on to www.bookweb.org.

Reaching across Your Region

Regional associations around the country — all of which are independent from ABA but work cooperatively with the national association on many initiatives — vary dramatically in breadth, scope, and offerings. Many offer their own trade shows, which are business, social, and cultural events. Larger regional shows are like mini-BEAs: great educational offerings, opportunities to meet publishers and look over their goods, and a chance to meet with authors.

To find the regional association nearest you, log on to www.bookweb.org, click on Organizations & Events, and then click on Regional Booksellers Associations.

Although BEA gives you a great opportunity to raise the profile of your store with the head honchos of publishers' sales and marketing divisions, in the smaller format of a regional tradeshow, you can catch up with your own sales reps and see new books from local publishers who may not attend BEA. For many booksellers, this blend of socializing with colleagues while also placing orders and getting some business done is a once-a-year pleasure.

Regional bookselling associations also look for ways to promote books and bookselling in their regions. Some associations produce catalogs, others host book festivals, and a number of regional associations publish regional Book Sense Bestseller Lists that reflect the unique tastes of each region.

If you're interested in becoming an active contributor in the bookselling community, your regional association is a great place to start. Get in touch with the president and executive director in your area, and let them know you'd like to serve on a committee or board.

An offering from at least one of the regional bookselling associations is *book doctors,* booksellers with particular expertise (events, personnel, buying, used books, and so on) who are on-call for all regional booksellers.

No Book Burning! Taking a Stand on the First Amendment

The American Booksellers Foundation for Free Expression (ABFFE) is an organization of booksellers that promotes and defends first amendment rights. The group's primary event is the sponsorship of Banned Book Week in late September, an event in which booksellers around the country display, read from, celebrate, and promote books that were once banned — really radical titles like *Black Beauty, Tom Sawyer, The Call of the Wild, The Canterbury Tales,* and Whitman's *Leaves of Grass.* If banning that short list makes your blood boil, you need to be a member of ABFFE.

Muggles for Harry Potter

In 2000, ABFFE started a Web site called Muggles for Harry Potter, a place where kids could defend Harry Potter books, which were banned in some public schools. Today, the site, which is now called kidsSPEAK!, is sponsored by the ABFFE, the National Coalition Against Censorship, the Association of American Publishers, and a number of other groups. For stunning examples of recent censorship in public schools and other kids' venues, go to `www.kidspeak online.org` and click on kidSPEAK News!

The organization does much more than sponsor Banned Book Week; it also:

✔ Monitors free speech issues and urges Congress, state legislatures, and booksellers to oppose bills that restrict free speech

✔ Educates the public about the importance of free speech

✔ Raises money and submits briefs for lawsuits that, among other things, block search warrants by police departments trying to gain access to customers' records

✔ Serves as a source of news about issues of free expression

✔ Promotes a free exchange of ideas and writings, especially by voices that don't share the predominant view

You can become a member of ABFFE for $35 per year for you individually ($100 for your store). Visit ABFFE online at `www.abffe.org`.

One More Resource: This Book

You have one more friend in the bookselling biz that's worth a mention in this chapter: this book. Just as ABA, your regional bookselling association, and ABFFE are resources for you to turn to in need, this book also offers advice, practical tips, and interesting bookselling techniques that were collected from booksellers around the country.

The following sections show you just how handy of a reference guide this book is.

Redefining your mission

You need a mission for your store and a vision of where it's headed. Oh, sure: You probably developed a mission statement years ago and have it sitting in a dusty frame on your office wall, right? Time to take it down, blow off the dust, and take a good, long look at it again. The bookselling industry has changed, and so should your store if you want to retain (and even increase) your share of the market. Take a peek at Chapter 2 and get a road map for where your store is headed.

Seeking new (and keeping existing) customers

To keep your business healthy, you need to hang on to your current customers, find out why some customers are choosing not to buy from you, and develop new customers to expand your business. For help pinning down why customers buy — and why they don't — flip to Chapter 3.

Taking a hard look at your categories

Your store's categories and sidelines need some *futzing* from time to time: expanding categories and sidelines that work for your store and contracting the ones that don't. Even if you developed a perfect mix of categories as recently as six months ago, you still want to look at your sales numbers (category by category) and make some hard decisions about which sections to keep and which to return to publishers. Books are subject to the winds of change as much as high couture is, so you need to continuously revisit your categories — perhaps as often as once a month — and make sure that they're profitable for your bookshop. See Chapter 4.

Effectively managing your inventory

Managing your inventory wisely — from the way you order frontlist titles to your method of keeping backlist books on your shelves; from used books to remainders; from choosing a new inventory control system to making returns — is what separates a healthy, growing bookshop from a sickly, on-its-last-legs store. Chapters 5 and 6 share much more detail about managing inventory.

Selling books: Merchandising, improving traffic, and handselling

You get only one chance to make a first impression, so think of the mood and décor of your store (discussed in Chapter 7) as one of the lures that draws customers in the doors and makes them decide to stay when they get there. In Chapter 8, you find a bundle of ways to start a buzz about your store, including tips for generating free publicity, using your Web site and e-mail to send electronic newsletters and postcards, staging killer events that attract gobs of people, making your store the center of your community, and tapping into the powerful program from ABA called Book Sense.

Chapter 9 helps you sell more effectively, from knowing what to say when customers walk in the door to taking advantage of corporate and institutional sales opportunities.

Building a Web site

Chapter 10 helps you build a hip Web site that'll connect you with all of your Generation X and Generation Y customers — and before long, with every single customer you have, both young and young at heart. You find out how BookSense.com provides you with easy, foolproof tools to get your Web site up and running in under 12 hours.

Managing employees

Managing your employees is never easy, but Chapter 11 helps you attract your ideal employees, interview effectively, get them to stick around (at least semi-permanently), train your employees to best represent you and your store, and give frequent feedback to each employee so that they keep doing things right and improve on weak areas.

Doing taxes and keeping financials

Do you dread paperwork? Chapters 12 and 13 may not be a barrel of laughs, but they can improve your understanding of taxes and financial statements.

Chapter 2

Business Planning 101: Redefining Who You Are

● ●

In This Chapter

▶ Going on a vision quest

▶ Deciding what your shop is trying to achieve

▶ Looking at your competition

▶ Dealing with that dreaded word: *financials*

▶ Putting together a working business plan

● ●

C hances are, the bookselling landscape today looks radi-
cally different from when you first opened your shop.
Chain bookstores (both online and in your local shopping
plaza), discount price clubs, Internet booksellers, and mass
merchandisers are all seeking your customers, and in an effort
to tighten their own financial belts, your customers may be
taking the bait.

This ever-increasing competition doesn't mean that you throw
in the towel and watch helplessly while other retailers take
over the bookselling biz. It may mean, however, that you
revisit what you and your store are trying to achieve by being
in business as an independent bookseller. It also definitely
means that you take a long, hard look at your competition —
both online and in your immediate geographic area — to
determine what you can do to retain your existing customers
and to expand your customer base.

Even if you don't have any need for a formal business plan (as you do if you're thinking about qualifying for a loan to expand your existing store, buy your building, or open another bookshop), the brainstorming and step-by-step instructions in this chapter help you to boldly face your competition and meet it head-on.

Assessing the Bookselling Business Environment

If your bookstore faces no competition, enjoys high *margins* (the difference between your sales and your expenses), and allows you to work a part-time schedule while still making a terrific living, you can skip this section.

But chances are, your store faces ever-increasing competition — from Internet sales, bookstore chains, wholesale clubs that sell books only as a small percentage of their businesses, or even from other independent booksellers in your area. You face some hard realities: low margins, high payroll costs, expensive rent, and declining sales. Consider the following numbers derived from ABA's preliminary ABACUS study, which at the time of publication included the date from about 110 independent bookshops. (As the ABACUS project develops, the numbers may change a bit.)

- On average, for every $100 in independent bookshop sales, about $59.20 goes for merchandise and freight.

- About $8.80 is spent on occupancy (rent, utilities, and other costs of maintaining a storefront location).

- About $20.70 goes to payroll (compensation, benefits, and other costs of hiring and retaining employees, including your own salary).

- That leaves $11.30 to cover all other operating expenses, including everything from advertising and Web site maintenance to packing tape and paper towels. To see a profit, you have to run a tight ship, with an eye toward maximizing every sales opportunity, while keeping costs well under control.

A little depressing, huh? Sure. But if you're developing a business plan, you have to face these realities head on, because every plan requires an honest rendering of the marketplace. With necessity being the mother of invention, knowing that you're facing a difficult market makes you more aware of every dollar spent, more creative in how you attract business, and more enthusiastic when you're successful.

The remaining sections in this chapter help you chart a course for thriving in the bookselling business.

Mission Possible: Your Store's Mission and Vision

Even if you think mission and vision statements are absolute hooey — and many that hang on the walls of small businesses and large corporations are — take a stroll through this section. You may find that developing a mission statement and daydreaming about your vision of the bookshop in the future is exactly what you need to jump-start your business.

To keep from confusing mission and vision, consider the following definitions:

- ✔ A *mission statement* defines what your business is and what you do for customers. (What is your mission today?)
- ✔ A *vision statement* describes where you want your business to go in the future. (What is your vision of tomorrow?)

To find out even more about mission and vision statements — and about business plans in general — check out *Business Plans For Dummies* by Paul Tiffany and Steven Peterson, or the more hands-on version, *Business Plans Kit For Dummies,* by Steven Peterson and Peter Jared (both by Wiley Publishing, Inc.).

Crafting a mission statement

Does the mere mention of the term "mission statement" make you roll your eyes? Do you immediately think of what an utter waste of time these statements are? For many businesses, you're right on target, because mission statements have gotten pretty out of hand. Everyone develops them, yet only a few pay attention to them.

A typical mission statement is nonsense: Four or five sentences that try to be so all-inclusive that they don't help the business narrow its focus or target key customers. You've probably seen something along the lines of the following statement:

> *ABC Business strives to create value for our customers by offering high-quality, low-cost products and services that are sold in a respectful environment by valued members of the team who work for dedicated management that strives to create the most value for stockholders.*

The mission statement is then framed and placed front and center — in the company's entryway, break room, bathrooms, offices, and so on. Customers and employees read it, scratch their heads, and go on with their daily routines without skipping a beat.

So the question is, what does a mission statement do for the business? The answer? Practically nothing. That's right: A final mission statement does nearly zippo for your business, but the *process of writing it* can affect great change within your bookshop. The greatest value in a mission statement isn't found in the framed document; rather, the strength of a mission statement comes from creating it, when you force yourself to face difficult realities about your business, your customers, your competitors, and your future.

Unless you essentially run your bookshop entirely by yourself, be careful that you don't create a mission statement in a vacuum. Instead, ask your employees to share their ideas in one or more meetings in which you encourage frank discussion. The more you involve your staff in the creation of your mission, the more motivated they will be to make the mission possible. You may also want to invite a few of your most valued customers to participate in framing your bookshop's mission statement.

To begin defining your business and how it serves customers' needs, get your staff together after you close for the evening, serve refreshments and snacks, and begin jotting down everyone's answers to the following questions:

✔ What products and services do we offer?

✔ What geographic area do we serve?

✔ How do we describe our best customers?

✔ What customer needs do we satisfy?

✔ Who is our competition? What do we know about them? What, if any, advantages do they offer over our store?

- Other independent booksellers in the area?

- Internet-based booksellers and book clubs?

- National bookstore chain store(s)?

- Price clubs?

- Mass merchandisers?

- Drugstores, grocery stores, airport vendors?

- Other?

✔ How does our store differ from the competition?

✔ What value do our differences hold for our customers?

✔ What brings a customer back to our store?

Based on the answers to the preceding questions, you can begin to define your store, review its strengths, and identify the needs you currently meet (and want to meet in the future) within your community. Here's an example of a beginning mission statement that could emerge after you've distilled your answers to the preceding questions down a bit:

Archetype Bookshop is an all-purpose bookshop offering books, magazines, newspapers, stationery, and greeting cards to the Lake Township community, an area with approximately 30,000 residents. We define our customers as people of all incomes, educational levels, and ages who love to read a wide variety of books. Our customers visit the store because our staff is extremely knowledgeable, friendly, and responsive to their needs. We offer a level of service that price clubs cannot match, and by joining our Frequent-Buyer Club, our product prices are in line with that of the national bookstore chains and Internet bookstores.

Scoping out the competition

If you aren't sure what potential customers see in your competition, visit the competition in person or online. Visit Amazon.com and other Internet sellers to check out their selection, prices, shipping rates and timelines, and return policies. Join an Internet book club, such as Quality Paperback Book Club (QPBC), to determine how you can compete with its products and services. Venture into your local Barnes & Noble or Borders store and research what they do — and don't — offer their customers. If you don't have a price-club membership, go with a friend who does and check out their book selection. Visit Wal-Mart, Kmart, Target, and other mass merchandisers to check out their displays and products. Every piece of information you gather by scoping out your competition helps you to better focus your shop's products and services.

If you don't plan to post your mission statement, you can stop there. You've thought hard about who you are, what you do, and how you can compete, and you can move on to envisioning your bookstore in the future and setting goals and objectives for your bookshop.

If, on the other hand, you want to display your mission statement — and many people do this as a daily reminder of why they're in business — trim it down to 50 words or less. Leave in anything that helps you remember what you do and for whom you do it and take out whatever isn't as relevant on a day-to-day basis. Here's an example:

Archetype Bookshop is a gathering place for readers of all incomes, educational levels, and ages. Our customers visit the store because our staff is extremely knowledgeable, friendly, and responsive to their needs, and we offer a level of service that our competition cannot match.

Envisioning your future

Close your eyes and picture your store two, five, or ten years into the future:

✔ **Where is your future store located (which area of your town)?** Are you in the same store, or have you moved?

✔ **What does the store's exterior look like?** Is this a simple, country bookshop with a bright-red awning or a lavish storefront with pillars and mahogany wood accents?

✔ **What do you see inside the shop?** What additional selection or services do you offer? How spacious is the store? How do customers move throughout the store? Which sections are most important? What sidelines do you sell?

✔ **How are your employees and customers interacting?** Do your customers linger? Do they use your store for meetings or purposes other than book-browsing? Are employees knowledgeable and respectful? Does your Web site extend the reach of your bookshop? What else about your customers or employees can you picture or imagine?

✔ **What receiving, storage, office, or meeting areas does your future bookshop offer?** How do you see these areas meshing with the rest of the store and the ordering and inventory systems you envision?

When you can begin to answer these questions, you have a *vision statement* that can guide your future decisions. Here's an example:

> *In our new, 2,000-square-foot location in a building we own in downtown Lake City, Archetype Bookshop offers pastries and hot beverages in addition to books, magazines, newspapers, stationery, and greeting cards. Our customers include the 30,000 residents of Lake Township, but through our extensive Internet site, we also serve a portion of the additional 100,000 visitors to our township each summer. Our bookstore is a daily gathering place for our local customers, who come in for coffee and pastries as a part of their daily routine; our employees know each local customer by name. In our large meeting room downstairs, customers join our many book clubs, hold company and community meetings, and take yoga classes.*

Growing without pains

Ed and Barbara Morrow started Northshire Bookstore in 1976 with about 1,000 square feet of retail space. With time, the store's square footage grew to over 5,000. Before long, however, Northshire Books reached an awkward stage in growth: The store was too large to be a mom-and-pop store but too small to be able to hire the support (back-office) staff they needed in order to grow larger. So, Northshire made the strategic decision to grow, both to allow for more customers and to support a larger — yet still well-paid — staff.

The Morrows identified some key areas on which to focus their growth:

✔ **Identify new products to sell:** Which sidelines and book categories could they bring in to support the main mission (selling books)? Could they expand existing profitable product lines (such as music)?

✔ **Improve margins on existing products:** Where were the inefficiencies? The Morrows stepped back and thought about how they would run the store if they were starting from scratch — and then they revamped their inefficient processes.

✔ **Develop a better facility:** The Morrows identified the optimal retail space for their store and compared it to what they could afford. In addition to increasing retail space, Northshire decided to add a café, a feature that customers of larger bookstores have come to expect.

✔ **Hire support staff that will allow the store to grow:** The more employees are available to coordinate events, go off-site for additional bookselling opportunities, and take over some of the book-buying duties, the more the store can grow, so the Morrows hired a support staff. And, in order to support that staff and pay them well, the store *has* to grow!

✔ **Consider opening a second store in the future:** The location has to be one that can share certain synergies with the current store: advertising, management, store name, and so on.

After lots of strategy sessions and careful financial planning, the Morrows are expanding the store to add a café, another 6,000 square feet of retail space, and additional parking. They'll build the addition first, and when that space is finished, move into it and close off the existing space to remodel it. They also plan to open another store after they finish the remodel. By spreading their increased management and buying costs across a larger operation, they will achieve better profitability.

Make sure your vision statement is realistic. If your store is located in a rural community of 5,000 people and you envision a 10,000-square-foot store, the reality of your current customer base and the one you hope to attract may be too far apart for your vision to come to pass. Think positively, but realistically.

Although you do want to involve your staff in crafting your vision statement, keep in mind that some staffers — for example, the third-year chemical engineering student who works part time — may not care as much about the future of the store as you do. That said, crafting a vision statement is much like creating a mission statement: The more people you invite into the process, the more people support you in making your vision a reality.

A vision statement is an especially helpful starting point if you're thinking of making a change in your business: moving, adding another store, remodeling, expanding, offering new products and/or services, and so on. Before taking the first steps toward making that change, develop a vision statement by writing down the dream inside your head.

Identifying Your Store's Strengths and Weaknesses

Do you remember the last time you worked for someone else, and you were reviewed periodically by your boss? You got a lot of positive feedback, right? But perhaps you also heard one or two pieces of negative feedback about the area in which you needed to improve. And, no matter how much good news you heard, the bad news stabbed like a knife in your heart.

I wish I could tell you that this section is nothing like those old days, and that reviewing your store's strengths and weaknesses is a barrel of fun. But because you're examining strengths *and* weaknesses, you're bringing your store's weaknesses out in the open — on paper, no less — and that's likely to bring you some pain. Ah, but with pain comes growth, right? This section gives you an opportunity to give your bookshop an unflinchingly honest appraisal. Are you ready?

To identify your strengths and weaknesses, complete the questionnaire in Table 2-1 — and be as honest as possible!

Table 2-1	Strengths and Weaknesses			
Areas of Importance	*How Your Bookshop Scores*			
Our location	Poor	Fair	Good	Excellent
Staying current with new products	Poor	Fair	Good	Excellent
General product knowledge	Poor	Fair	Good	Excellent
Ordering products	Poor	Fair	Good	Excellent
Managing inventory	Poor	Fair	Good	Excellent
Merchandising	Poor	Fair	Good	Excellent
Staging events	Poor	Fair	Good	Excellent
Selling	Poor	Fair	Good	Excellent
Customer service	Poor	Fair	Good	Excellent
Working with the community	Poor	Fair	Good	Excellent
Managing our Web site	Poor	Fair	Good	Excellent
Hiring and retaining employees	Poor	Fair	Good	Excellent
Paying bills and managing paperwork	Poor	Fair	Good	Excellent
Bottom line profitability	Poor	Fair	Good	Excellent

Table 2-1 is a review of the skills and capabilities of *everyone* in your store. So, if you're terrific at sales, but you're on the floor infrequently and the rest of your staff loathes selling to customers, your store has a weakness.

Determining Your Goals and Objectives

Does your mission statement fall short — even just slightly short — of the day-in, day-out realities of running your bookstore? Does your vision seem improbable because you have a long way to go before your bookshop begins to resemble the one you've envisioned? Do you want to insulate yourself from threats and improve on your weaknesses?

No bookstore is perfect, and no one expects yours to be, but if you see a gap between where you are and where your business needs to be to compete, put new business goals and objectives into place. Here's how:

1. **Identify key phrases in your mission (or vision) statement, threats or opportunities in your industry, or weaknesses in your store.**

   For example, the Archetype Bookshop mission statement identifies the following key phrases:

   - Our staff is extremely knowledgeable.

   - Our staff is friendly.

   - Our staff is responsive.

2. **Develop a goal for each key phrase.**

   In this example, each of Archetype Bookshop's key phrases is given a goal:

   - **Key phrase:** Our staff is extremely knowledgeable.

     Goal: Expose the staff to as many new books as possible.

   - **Key phrase:** Our staff is friendly.

     Goal: Encourage the staff to memorize customers' names.

   - **Key phrase:** Our staff is responsive.

     Goal: Train the staff to try always to meet the customers needs by checking all possible areas of the store for inventory and by taking special orders.

3. Develop an objective for the first goal.

An *objective* is a tangible task that you can put on and cross off of your To-Do List. An objective should always be achievable in a specific time frame.

For Archetype's first goal — expose the staff to as many new books as possible — the bookshop develops the following objectives:

- Hold weekly (paid) meetings at which staff members discuss what they're reading.

- Assign Ellen to maintain up-to-date copies of *Publisher's Weekly* and the *New York Times Book Review* in the break room, and also find and print out online book reviews from specific Web sites, such as Book Sense, PW Daily for Booksellers, Publisher's Lunch, Holt Uncensored, and Bookselling This Week (see Chapter 6 for details on these sites).

- Assign Hank to post daily listings of broadcast schedules from PW Daily, I-Page, and Bookselling This Week, and ask employees to check the listings before going on the sales floor.

- Assign Brian to secure as many copies of galleys as possible and ask for staff volunteers to read and review them.

- Send Adrian, the book buyer, to BookExpo America (BEA) and follow up with one or two meetings for the entire staff to get the scoop.

- Send all interested booksellers to the regional trade show and ask them to report back at staff meetings.

4. Attach "do by" dates to each objective and establish periodic reviews of the objectives.

Each week, month, or other time frame that works for you, check the status of each objective. Before long, your bookshop's day-to-day reality will begin to match your business and community mission, as well as that vision of your future store.

New Words for an older store

New Words Bookstore — a women's bookshop — opened in 1974, just at the beginning of both the feminist movement and independent publishing endeavors by women. For 15 straight years, sales shot up, and the store became a meeting place for women in Cambridge, Boston, and across New England. In the early 1990s, when larger publishers and general stores began to embrace books for and about women, sales at this specialty store began to level off, and, more recently, to drop precipitously. The store's location, once at the hub of feminist activity, was on the outskirts of urban life. The women's movement, bookselling as a profession, the publishing industry, and even the owners had changed dramatically in the nearly 30 years since the bookstore had opened. The owners, who no longer felt like a part of the community in the same way they had been and who wanted to find a way to be vital and magnetic again, needed to rethink the store's vision.

With help from the Ford Foundation, New Words spent a year researching the cultural role of women's bookstores in their communities. New Words wanted to keep its own bookstore from dying, keep the employees motivated, and maintain its community activist vision. As a result of its research, the store is undergoing a transition: The owners have begun to design the Center for New Words, a nonprofit organization that will encourage women's and girls' writing

and offer a small bookstore within it. Because the owners didn't want to endanger their place in the community or compromise their values, they determined that the first step would be to close the bookstore during the transition, while they still remained in good financial standing with their suppliers. So, New Words closed and successfully paid off its creditors, which means that the store's name and excellent reputation remain intact among colleagues, publishers, and customers. Now, during the transition between old and new, the owners continue to hold events, order books for those events and for the store's book club, and answer the store's phone line.

The community is enthusiastic that the Center, when it opens, will still combine reading, writing, and women, and will play a central role in the community. For example, the Center is considering a future partnership with a transitional women's shelter in which the Center and the shelter would ask local book clubs to read a specific book about domestic violence. The Center would then co-sponsor an event that would bring together the author of that book, women who have been served by the shelter, and book club members to engage in meaningful discussion. This is one way that the owners of New Words hope to transform their bookstore that became unprofitable into a vital and profitable place for women and the surrounding community.

You may decide to tackle just one phrase of your mission statement at a time. That's fine. What's important is that you follow through and monitor your progress. When you're ready, proceed to the next key phrase in your statement. Remember, a mission unaccomplished doesn't help you, your staff, your customers, or your business. If you let your mission and vision sit, they become just another meaningless exercise.

Sketching Out a Business Plan

Because you're already in business, you may decide that you don't need a formal business plan. However, if you approach your lender for an increase in your credit line, to refinance your business loan, or for a new loan to remodel or expand, the lender's going to require a business plan from you. Some bookstores also seek investors or invite a new partner to participate in a major expansion. Have a business plan in place before you approach any potential funder, whether that's an institution or an individual. If you've already read through much of this chapter, you have most of the information that goes into a business plan:

- ✓ **Executive summary:** This one-page summary of the plan is the last piece you draft. Think of this page as the CliffsNotes version of your business plan.

  Don't make an executive summary longer than one page. Chances are, the person reading it will stop at one page anyway, regardless of how much you write.

- ✓ **Bookselling environment:** This part of your plan discusses trends and statistics about the bookselling industry. How much money do people spend on books? At what sort of stores do they buy them? Is the book-buying trend up or down? This information can change quickly, so keep it up-to-date. Use the American Bookselling Association Web site, www.bookweb.org, as a resource for this information and follow the studies published in trade magazines, in print and online. Also, take a look at the "Assessing the Bookselling Business Environment" section earlier in this chapter for a feel for some of those numbers.

✔ **Bookshop overview and description:** This part describes your store in detail and includes the following information:

- Mission and vision statements

- A description of your products and services, including your unique niche in the marketplace

- A description of your inventory, computer system, fixtures, as well as features of your location

- Bios of your store's employees, highlighting unique and important skills

- Strengths that show advantages over competitors

- Analysis of your customers (see Chapter 3)

✔ **Financial overview:** This part includes the big-three standard financial statements: income statement, balance sheet, and profit-and-loss statement. Some lenders may also ask for a cash-flow statement. See Chapter 13 for the lowdown on all these financial documents.

✔ **Strategy or action plan:** This segment discusses your go-forwards and may list your goals and objectives, discuss your weaknesses and how you plan to turn them into strengths, and review your major competitors and how you plan to compete with them.

What you're doing here is soothing fears. Lenders and others reading your business plan want to know that you have your eyes open, you've identified your bookshop's weaknesses, and you're addressing them.

This isn't so bad, is it? A business plan isn't a document you throw together in an hour or two, but it also doesn't have to require weeks or months of your time. Spending some time developing a strong business plan, even if you never use it to obtain external funding, will surely strengthen your bookshop and help you hit a home run with any new curveball that comes your way.

Chapter 3

Figuring Out What Customers Want

*W*ooing and retaining customers is one of the most challenging aspects of any retail business. Businesses with loyal customers meet — and more importantly, *anticipate* — their customers' needs. Doing so isn't an easy job for any retailer, but it's especially difficult for booksellers. Not only do your customers' needs change, but so do your products. You have to peruse thousands of new titles each year and evaluate whether those new books will generate customer demand.

This chapter helps you gather information from your customers, think in terms of their needs, figure out why some people don't buy from you, and make your bookshop stand out in the eyes of your customers.

Getting to Know You, Getting to Know All about You

Of course you know your customers. You can recognize most of them by name as they walk through your doors, and you know a little about each one.

However, the information you've gleaned from your customers may be sketchy and not well documented. For example, you may know that Mrs. Buysalot has several grandchildren, but you may not know their ages, where they live, or what sort of books they prefer. If you did know that information, you could help Mrs. Buysalot buy birthday and holiday gifts by suggesting certain new books that tend to appeal to kids of a certain age, gender, and geographic center.

What are your customers like?

To divide your customers into groups or market segments, you need to examine your customers from a variety of different angles. You want to know the following about your customers and about the people for whom your customers buy gifts:

- ✔ Neighborhood or other geographic area
- ✔ Hobbies
- ✔ Gender
- ✔ Preferred authors
- ✔ Reading level
- ✔ Age
- ✔ Political leanings
- ✔ Religious underpinnings
- ✔ Preferred language
- ✔ Family or marital status
- ✔ Vacation preference
- ✔ Income

Obviously, you're not going to be able to come right out and ask your customers most of these questions, except, perhaps, the first four or five. However, by developing a system to track which books and sidelines customers buy and which events they attend, you may be able to ascertain these answers indirectly.

Tracking and targeting customers intelligently

If you're like many booksellers, you segment your customers based on certain assumptions and bits and pieces of information. You think you know who your customers are, but the information is more from a gut feel than from research.

One bookshop owner, for example, believed the majority of her customers were Hispanic Americans, so the shop sent out a newsletter and created signs in Spanish, stocked a wide range of Spanish-language books, and hired Spanish/English bilingual employees. What market research told them, however, was that an equally large percentage of their customers were Vietnamese Americans. Although employees where surprised by that information, the shop was able to react quickly, stocking Vietnamese-language books and beginning to find ways to better communicate with Vietnamese American customers.

Rather than guessing about your customers interests in order to make the best business decisions for your bookshop, develop a *system* of knowing what your customers want to buy. Here's how:

- ✔ **Develop a method** of identifying your customers, finding out about their interests, tracking their purchases, and providing them with information that's appropriate for them.

- ✔ **Give customers a reason to give you the information you need to develop this method.** Many bookshops initiate a membership or customer-loyalty program, in which customers voluntarily fill out information cards or give information verbally to booksellers in exchange for a gift certificate or other reward. One bookshop gives one percent of customers' purchases to charities of the customers' choice.

- ✔ **Use a database** to store and retrieve the information you collect. Ideally, the database should capture information at your point of purchase — many inventory programs offer this option. These systems allow you to track your customers' purchases as they make them and review customer and sales data as often as you like.

If your software doesn't offer this feature, you can create your own database. At a minimum, a database will store the name, address, phone number, and e-mail address of each customer, but ideally, you can also track gift purchases, favorite authors, book club memberships, special orders, sideline preferences, café buying trends, and event attendance.

If your store and/or computer system isn't big enough for one of the monstrously powerful databases, such as Access, FoxPro, or FileMaker Pro, a spreadsheet like Excel may give you all the power and flexibility you need to manage your data.

The U.S. Postal Service (USPS) offers a low-cost database-cleaning service that deletes old addresses, standardizes addresses to meet USPS requirements, and adds ZIP+4 codes. You simply send the USPS your database, and you get it back, all cleaned up. Contact your local postmaster for information — and think of all the money you'll save avoiding returned mailings. See Chapter 8 for tips on sending mailings to customers and potential customers.

If you implement a system like this, the result is called *targeted marketing:* You inform customers about the products, events, and services that they're likely to be interested in, and you don't bother them with any other information. You discover entire areas of interest that you didn't know existed before, and you can leverage those interests into business opportunities. You also find out which customers are falling into the *80/20* rule — they take up 80 percent of your time but bring in only 20 percent of your business — and you find ways to encourage them to become more profitable for you.

Targeted marketing also helps you sharpen your buying, strengthen how you manage your inventory, and improve how you handsell books to customers (see Chapter 9 for more on handselling).

A targeted mailing generates more interest from publishers than an untargeted mailing does. If you can show a publisher that you can promote a particular book to the right target market, you may get a larger chunk of the co-op money that you've earned to use for that promotion.

Getting ABA's help

If you don't know a market segment from a marmalade scone, you may be able to get help from a special ABA program called LMI. LMI stands for *Local Marketing Intelligence*, and it's available to ABA bookstore members and individuals interested in opening a bookstore. LMI works with you to find ways to attract new customers by helping you analyze and act on your current customer data. The program allows you to determine which ZIP codes within your local area offer the best marketing potential and helps you figure out how to reach the customers who live there. In a nutshell, you find out which market segments fit best with your store's mission and vision (refer to Chapter 2) and which will likely be a drain on your time and energy. For details, visit www.bookweb.org and click on Products and Services. Then click on LMI.

Keeping data private

Is your first reaction to the idea of digging for data one of fear — fear that you'll know too much about your customers and inadvertently violate their trust? Do you worry about being in the situation of Denver's Tattered Cover Book Store, in which you're asked to turn over potentially damaging information about a customer's buying habits — information that could result in a decade or more of jail time for your customer? Do you try to disconnect customers' names from what they buy to give them the most possible privacy?

If this sounds like you, think about storing and using information only on customers who have opted in to the program, so that you give customers the choice of whether to participate or steer clear.

Just because you use the information to better serve your customers doesn't mean you'll ever be compelled to turn it over to a third party. On your opt-in card, make customers aware of your privacy policy, pledging to take meticulous care of their information and always respecting the privacy of their choices of books and other products. Be sure readers also know that you'll never sell your information or disclose purchase patterns to anyone, including the government, without the consent of your customers. As one bookseller puts it, "We're the Swiss bank of bookstores."

For additional information about privacy issues, including more on the Tattered Cover case, visit ABFFE's Web site at www.abffe.org.

Looking for a "Need"-le in a Haystack

Ultimately, every customer who buys from you does so because you're meeting a need in that person. These needs run the gamut:

- **A need for survival:** Although books hardly seem to fit on the same level as food, clothing, and shelter, when a customer comes in for a title about interviewing for a job, needs a plumbing book in a hurry, looks for a good book on budgeting or debt management, or wants a book about canning garden vegetables, you're filling a very basic need. At this level, the books you sell to customers are enhancing careers that supply money to meet basic needs or are teaching skills that also allow customers to meet those needs.

- **The need for belonging and acceptance:** Everyone needs to belong to some group and to feel loved and accepted there. You may be filling this need by having established a bookshop where customers feel welcomed and as though they're among friends. You may coordinate book clubs that make members feel a sense of belonging with other like-minded people. You may help a customer choose a title that helps him or her dress or behave in a way that's more socially acceptable.

- **The need for achievement and fulfillment:** This, too, is a strong — and often unmet — need in society. You may sell test-prep or school-equivalency books that help customers get a diploma or degree. A French-language book-and-tape set you sell may be just the encouragement a customer needs to learn a new language. A book on fitness or dieting may turn a person's life around. An investment book may allow a customer to retire early and start an entirely new career direction. Children's books may help your young customers master all sorts of reading and life skills.

- **The need for understanding — of yourself and those around you:** Many of the books you sell fall into this category. From books about Islam to titles about how to parent teenagers, you're selling knowledge that helps the world get along just a little better. Self-help books, too, help your

customers better understand themselves, just as preg-
nancy books help both husband and wife understand the
physical changes the woman is going through. Also, don't
forget the insights readers gain from great literature —
whether classic or contemporary.

✔ **The need for relaxation and entertainment:** Although
Americans are faced with more entertainment options
than ever before, they also work longer hours and have
less time to enjoy themselves. By putting a hot new novel
into a customer's hands, you've helped him or her relax,
even if just for a few hours. By selling travel guides,
you've encouraged a much-needed vacation. By scheduling Saturday morning story time, you've entertained a
group of grade-schoolers.

Think of it this way: You're not selling books, you're meeting
customers' needs! Chapter 9 tells you how to fill these needs
effectively as you work with customers.

Figuring Out Why You're Not a Customer's Cup of Tea

Suppose half of the people who come into your store buy a
product before leaving. You may be thinking that you're doing
pretty well, getting 50 percent to buy. The reality is that even if
half of all your browsers buy, the other half is looking at your
store and your selection, experiencing your service, and then
walking away. Why is that?

Understanding why some people *don't* buy is a difficult under-
taking. After all, your competitors' customers aren't going to
drop by your store just to give you the lowdown on why they
buy at a price club or the nearest chain store. But you may be
able to get inside their heads, nonetheless, by taking these
steps.

1. **Spend time at your competitors' locations.**

   If you don't have time to do this yourself, you can ask
   staff members to help you and report back at the next
   store meeting. If possible, though, check out the competition with your own ears and eyes and add your
   impressions to those of your employees.

2. **Observe customers shopping for books at other bookstores, including chain stores, price clubs, and mass merchandisers.**

3. **Introduce yourself (so as not to frighten them), and ask whether they're willing to answer a few direct questions, such as:**

   - What factors led them to shopping here?

   - Are they planning to buy books here? Why or why not?

   - What do they like about the selection, or what would they change?

   - Do they shop elsewhere for books? Where?

4. **Listen carefully to the answers — and take notes!**

   Whatever you do, don't become defensive.

   Ask whether you can take their names and addresses in order to invite them to your store at a later date to test-drive some changes you may put in place. Or, ask them to volunteer to be a part of a focus group for your store that tests new products and services, in exchange for a store gift certificate.

5. **Let the notes percolate for a few days or weeks.**

   As soon as you're comfortable looking at all of the comments, pull out your scribbles and begin organizing them into two categories:

   - Those situations you may be able to address immediately. (You'll tackle these right away.)

   - Those changes that may take longer or, perhaps, can never be addressed. (Establish a date — three or six months in the future — when you'll pull these out and begin working on them.)

   You may decide that you have a third category — "problems" that you simply don't want to fix. Not all potential customers are good customers. If a person at a price club tells you he's buying there because the only factor that matters to him is price and deep discounts, perhaps you don't want to meet that customer's needs, now or in the future.

Keep in mind, however, that if you're answering every customer's concerns with, "Well, that's just not a customer I want," you're probably not being completely honest about your store's shortcomings.

6. **Get together with employees at your store, other booksellers with whom you are colleagues (ones you may meet at a workshop or conference, for example), or trusted family and friends, and begin to brainstorm ideas for addressing the easily addressable problems.**

   As with all brainstorming, be sure to consider every idea, no matter how kooky it may seem. By staying away from put-downs and seemingly harmless comments like, "that will never work," you encourage a vibrant and creative time to brainstorm.

7. **Put brainstormed corrections into place — even if you aren't sure that they'll work — and then invite your testers or focus group to evaluate them, if possible.**

   Ask your existing customers to comment on your changes, too, either with a small focus group or a written survey (both of which you reward with a gift certificate).

8. **Work on your longer-term, more difficult corrections at the appointed dates.**

9. **Repeat the information-gathering process at set dates, such as once a year.**

Are You Outstanding in the Field — or Standing Out in Left Field?

After you know what your customers are looking for, what sort of needs they want your bookshop to fill, and why certain customers have avoided buying from you in the past, then what do you do? How can you make your bookshop match your customers' interests, respond to your customers' needs, and draw new customers away from your competitors? You look at the four cornerstones of every bookshop: service, selection, location, and price.

Not just lip service

Service isn't just about how you greet customers as they walk into your store, although that's certainly a component. Service is about what you're willing to give to your customers in exchange for their patronage and loyalty:

- **How well do you remember the faces, names, and favorite books of your customers?** Service is about building a relationship — and a long-term one at that. Your goal is to sell your customers the last books they buy within their lifetimes. If you invest in each relationship by getting to know every customer and what he or she likes, your customers will support you.

  Many retailers treat customers like strangers to be endured rather than like friends with which to get acquainted.

- **What sort of atmosphere do you provide at your bookshop?** (See Chapter 7 for an entire chapter on your store's ambiance.) The beauty of running a community-based, independent bookstore is that you can make your store feel unique. You and your staff (along, perhaps, with a consultant you hire) get to draw from your community and create an atmosphere that fits you and your customers.

- **How knowledgeable are you are about books in general and the categories you carry in particular?** Your job is to make the best possible match between the books your customers want to read and the books you carry, and you do this by reading the books you carry. Sell customers only the best books for them — for example, you may find yourself telling a customer, "that book is good, but this one is great," even if the first book was more expensive or had a higher profit margin.

- **How well do you help book clubs manage their selections?** Book clubs aren't easy for club leaders to organize, and those leaders can often use your help. Can you spend time getting to know each leader's goals for the club and meeting to talk about potential book club selections? If club members come to depend on you for help in managing their selections, they also develop a sense of loyalty and respect for you and your booksellers. They're more likely to make their other book purchases at your store, as well.

✔ **How efficiently and quickly do you fill special orders?**
When customer service is of primary importance, special
orders are put into the ordering process immediately and
unpacked as soon as they arrive. You then call customers
right away to minimize their wait time.

You can build a loyal customer base just by meeting the
special needs of your customers, especially when your
selection doesn't match that of larger bookstores.

✔ **How quickly do you return phone calls?** Being busy
isn't a crime, so don't knock yourself out trying to return
every call within ten minutes, or even an hour. However,
do make sure that your respect for customers resonates
in how quickly and effectively you respond to their
requests for personal attention.

Customers can't often call the owner of a company and
get a quick response. Make yourself accessible, and your
customers will be loyal.

✔ **Which events do you offer and how well do those events
utilize your customers' precious time?** Chapter 8 gives
you the lowdown on events, but keep this in mind: Every
event should enhance your customers' lives and respect
the time they're giving up to attend the function. Keep feeling the pulse of your customers to make sure that your
events meet their needs and respect their time.

✔ **Do you provide additional free services, such as gift
wrapping, delivery, shipping, or gift registry?** Some
bookshops choose not to provide these services, but
when you do, customers are often thrilled — and immediately become more loyal. If a customer can pick up gifts
on the way to a birthday dinner or party and/or have gifts
delivered locally or shipped nationally, you've just shown
immense respect for that customer's time. A gift registry
is a newer idea, but an easy one to integrate with your
database: Kids can let you know which books they'd like
to get as gifts, and grandparents can come by to check
the registry and buy a few books from the list. Some
stores offer wedding registries, too — think of unabridged
dictionaries, atlases, and other books every new household should have! A birthday registry works for adults,
too — they can register their book desires with you and
make gift-buying easier for their family and friends.

✔ **How early do you open and how late do you close?** Most booksellers take one of two approaches: Stay open the same hours as the rest of the stores in the immediate area or stay open as late as the chain bookstores do. Neither approach allows the customer to impact the store's hours. Rather, use your database to determine when you're busiest, and then plan your core hours around those times. In addition, ask your customers — perhaps in a written survey — which hours would be convenient for them. If the majority of your customers visit your store during their lunch hours and after work but never in the morning, perhaps you can open at 11:00 a.m. and stay open later, rather than opening at 8:30 or 9:00 every morning and feeling beat by 5:00.

Selection: Giving 'em what they want

As an independent bookstore with a small bank account and limited shelf space, you need to decide whether you're an all-purpose bookstore or a specialty shop, and whether you carry new books only, used-only, or a combination of the two.

Establishing an all-purpose bookstore

An all-purpose store strives to carry titles in nearly every category: bestselling fiction and nonfiction, self-help, mysteries, sci fi, spiritual, computer books, professional and business books, university and small press books, art and architecture titles, foreign language, travel, cookbooks, children's books, local books — you name it! The upside of running an all-purpose store is that you can appeal to a large customer base. The downside is that, in order to fit all of those categories into your limited shelf space, you can't stock as many titles nor as many copies of the titles you carry.

Specializing in one or more book categories

Bookshops may specialize in almost any subject area: children's, travel, architecture and building, computer, foreign-language, literary, African American, women's, or sports books. Often, the area in which you're located dictates what sort of books you can carry (see the "Location, location, location" section that follows). Many stores start out as general stores, and by listening to their customers, decide to specialize in one or more of their subject areas. Their selection in one area may shrink while another category grows and thrives, all in response to customers' needs. The reverse can also be true: A children's bookstore begins by carrying book club titles to save time for busy moms, and then decides to experiment with a hand-picked selection of literary fiction, for example. If you listen to your customers and keep an open mind, some categories may take on a life of their own!

Carrying only new books or mixing new with used

For many years, booksellers followed a strict code of specializing in new books, used books, or old and rare books. A few of the larger bookstores dipped into more than one category, but they kept each type of book separate, sometimes even incorporating separate bookstore entrances for the new and used book areas.

Lately, however, a trend started by Powell's Books in Portland, Oregon, and used extensively at college textbook stores, has been picking up steam: *Integrate* new books with old, right on the bookstore shelves. Powell's — and the many other bookstores that have followed suit — now offers customers a powerful choice: Purchase a new, pristine book at full price or purchase the used book right next to it for far less money. Either way, the bookstore wins, because of the higher margins on used books (see Chapter 4) and the higher per-book profit on new books. Here's an example: A used book that sells for $7 may have cost just $1 to purchase, which is an 86 percent discount and a $6 gross profit. A new book that sells for $24 may have been purchased with only a 40 percent discount, but the book still makes a $9.60 gross profit. The customer wins, too, because he or she had the opportunity to get a $24 book for just $7 without making a separate trip to a used bookshop.

See Chapter 4 for more on deciding whether to carry used books.

Location, location, location

Back when chain bookstores were located only in malls and major metropolitan areas, independent bookshops in smaller markets had a tremendous opportunity to compete on location alone. Local customers could drive or walk to the store in ten minutes, rather than driving an hour to the nearest big city. But because the suburbs mushroomed and chain bookstores, mass merchandisers, and price clubs moved into mid-sized towns, you can no longer count on your location alone as a way to compete for customers.

So, you have two choices: Change your location or make the most of the one you're in by making sure that your selection matches the types of customers your area brings your way.

If you decide to change your location, that's terrific. Be prepared, however, to develop an entirely new business strategy for your store (refer to Chapter 2) and to lose many loyal customers in the transition (offset, you hope, by new customers in your new geographic area!).

For the most part, however, you're probably going to have to make the most of your current location. The following sections identify the most common bookstore locations.

Giving it the old college try

College towns offer unique possibilities for you to attract and retain customers:

- ✔ Recognize that your core customers are highly educated, socially active, and inclined to stock books that are unique to their sensibilities.

- ✔ Match your categories with specialty areas within the college or university. If your college has a specialized Ph.D. program in limericks of the Upine Tribe of South Central Pingali, make sure that you have a large category of that poetry in your store.

  Depending on the particular bent of the college in your area (strong in liberal arts, all-women's college, engineering school, strong business school, and so on), you may want to establish yourself as, for example, a literary bookstore, feminist bookshop, technical store, or business bookshop.

- ✔ Because so many of your customers are themselves published authors, hold a small party each time a professor publishes a book.

- ✔ Work your way into textbook business, which will generate significant additional volume for your store. As you develop relationships with professors who visit your store, ask for their textbook business.

> ✔ If appropriate, capitalize on the tourists who visit college towns by carrying sidelines that feature university logos. Be sure to spend time in the university bookstore to see how you can differentiate your sideline collection from the one offered there.

Bright lights, big city

As an urban bookseller, you may decide to stock a wide array of categories, especially if yours is the only bookstore in the downtown area. On the other hand, you may also have an opportunity to specialize your store to match the ethnic and religious diversity in your area and to be quite successful with that specialization.

Surrounding the cities: The 'burbs

A suburban bookstore has both limitations and extensive opportunities for specialization. Many suburban areas of the United States are still largely white and upper-middle class, which means that you're less likely to find success with a suburban bookshop that specializes in, for example, African American literature. However, you've also likely positioned your store in the middle of a highly educated group of people who value reading and education. Many suburban bookshops maintain a large children's section, for example, because they find that suburban parents want to spend money on books for their children.

Going on vacation: Rural/tourist area

A fourth category, rural areas, exists, but if your store fits this category, it's pretty rare. Most rural areas simply can't sustain the sales levels that even a small bookstore requires, unless the store is located in an area that swells from two to ten times its size during tourist seasons. If you're operating a bookshop in a tourist area, you make the majority of your income during the tourist season. During the off-season, you may cut back your hours substantially.

The key to running a successful tourist bookshop is to fill the needs of the tourists without forgetting the needs of the year-rounders. Visitors often have an idealized picture of your community in their minds, so think of books for them as souvenirs. If you live near the ocean or another large body of water, for example, carry books about water, boats, ships, beaches, beach houses, and so on. Be aware, however, that the year-rounders may have different interests entirely, so cater to them both on- and off-season. After all, their good word of mouth will bring summer (or winter) guests into your store. Many tourist bookshops also carry far more sidelines (see Chapter 4) than other bookshops do; some even create their own line of logo-wear so that the backs of their visiting customers promote their stores.

The price is right!

Price clubs, chain bookstores, and big Internet bookstores share a philosophy about price: Sell a high volume of items cheaply, and you'll make the same — or more — profit than if you sell a lower volume at a higher per-unit price.

Unfortunately, you can't compete with that, which doesn't mean, however, that you should throw in the towel and vow never to discount a title. Selective discounting works for many independent bookstores, particularly if you discount the books you think your customers will love. (Customers are more willing to take a risk on a recommendation if they aren't paying full price!) In place of direct discounting, other booksellers offer frequent-buyer clubs or reward their loyal customers.

Rainy Day Books in Fairway, Kansas, offers loyal customers a ten percent discount every day. New customers and people coming in to pick up tickets for off-site events are told about the discount in these words: "We offer our loyal Rainy Day Books customers a ten percent discount." Customers instantly recognize the emphasis on "loyal" and know that, in order to continue to get the discount, they need to make Rainy Day their only source for books.

You can't compete price for price with the big guys. So, think instead about competing with value. A book is worth more if you can give it a personal recommendation or deliver it the same day to your customer across town. Remind your customers of the breadth of services you offer. If you continually offer something of value to your customers, you may find them more willing to dig a little deeper into their pockets.

Part II
Managing Your Product

"Here's my business plan for the Jazz Store. I think we should just fake the budget, improvise the marketing and make up the long range goals as we go along."

In this part . . .

You take a look at the nuts and bolts of book buying —
deciding which categories are most appealing to your
audience, ordering the right products for your store, and
managing the inventory when it arrives. Here, you get the
scoop on frontlist titles, backlist titles, remainders, used
books, sidelines, and any other product you may order
and stock.

Chapter 4

Deciding What to Sell

· ·

In This Chapter

▶ Honing in on the types of books you want to carry

▶ Expanding and contracting categories

▶ Finding sidelines that complement your books — and make a great profit

· ·

So many books; so little space! No matter how large your store is, you can't carry every book in print. So how in the world does a red-blooded bookseller decide which of the thousands of books printed each year to stock and which to bypass? What about all those other book-related (or, not so related but cool-looking) products that you can order? How do you keep those items from overrunning your store?

Deciding what products to sell — and, perhaps, more importantly, what *not* to sell — is no easy task. However, this chapter is here to help by getting you to think in terms of book *categories,* or groupings, and to narrow down *sidelines,* those terrific products that supplement your book sales.

Understanding Various Book Categories

The categories you carry depend on the mission of your store (refer to Chapter 2), your geographic location, your customers' needs, and your own experience with particular authors, editors, and/or publishers. In short, you need to carry the categories that you think will sell well in your store! You're looking for a blend of books that work in your community and books that you and your staff feel passionate about. These titles differentiate your store from any other bookstore, because you're able to offer personal recommendations to your customers.

Your store can be as general or as specific as you want it to be, providing, of course, that your customers agree. Thinking of your own town, can you imagine a bookshop that successfully sells only poetry? In most areas, it just wouldn't happen. But the Grolier Poetry Book Shop in Cambridge, Massachusetts, does beautifully. In 1974, Louisa Solano took over the nearly 50-year-old bookshop and tried to continue its tradition as a general bookstore, but found that she had to specialize in order to compete with the abundance of other stores. Taking her direction from the current stock, she decided to specialize in poetry, and she hasn't looked back. Not only is the Grolier an integral part of the Boston area literary scene, but the store is also a destination for poets, writers, and visitors from around the world. Visit the store at `www.grolierpoetrybookshop.com`.

Fact or fiction: Books for grown-ups

Books for adults that are carried by bookstores can be divided into two broad subject areas: fiction (novels and short stories) and nonfiction (almost everything else). Within these broad areas, many booksellers carry what's thought of as standard fare.

Fiction

Fiction titles may fall into these categories:

- ✔ **Commercial fiction:** Novels with large print runs that publishers hope will make bestseller lists.

  A commercial author, like Stephen King, used to be a big seller at most independent bookstores. However, books by commercial authors are what price clubs hone in on, and as a result, some bookshops have pulled back on orders for these big-name authors. Consider focusing instead on books you can personally recommend to customers or titles vetted by other independent booksellers, like the Book Sense 76 (see Chapter 8).

- ✔ **Literary fiction:** Novels and short stories published with a smaller audience in mind.

✔ **Genre fiction:** Mysteries, science fiction and fantasy titles, romance, adventure fiction, and Westerns. How you break out and display these categories depends on what you can sell in your store. Although you can certainly base your decision on your own tastes, try not to be too snobby about what you consider to be "acceptable" fiction; your customers may like what you don't. (Think, especially, of romance fiction.) Mystery has been a hot category for many general stores and one to consider if you have an avid mystery reader on staff to make recommendations. Stores like the Mysterious Bookshop in New York City, New York, and Kate's Mystery Books in Cambridge, Massachusetts, specialize in crime fiction.

✔ **Classic fiction:** Novels, short stories, and other works by those writers considered to be masters. Some bookstores shelve these books alongside contemporary fiction; others prefer to keep classics in their own section. The classics tend to be the titles on school reading lists, so keeping them all in one section may prove easier for your customers.

Many booksellers use *adjacencies* (displaying similar categories close to each other) to promote browsing and to sell more books. For example, fiction is near mystery, parenting books are located near the children's section, and so on. This approach is similar to putting all the dairy products on the same aisle in the grocery store.

✔ **Poetry and drama:** Classic and contemporary poems and plays. Some purists argue that these books don't fall under the category of fiction, but if not strictly fiction, poetry and drama are at least kissing cousins.

Nonfiction

Nonfiction categories are usually grouped together in bookstores, with an eye for keeping books in clusters that make sense to the customer. For example:

✔ **General nonfiction:** Includes biography and memoir, history and politics, and books on current events and social issues.

✔ **Reference:** Includes English and foreign-language dictionaries, travel books, test guides, wedding planners, atlases and almanacs, and consumer guides.

✔ **Business reference:** May cover topics from personal finance to small-business management. Most stores also shelve computer and technology books near business reference.

✔ **Wellness:** Includes any books that fall into the categories of health, sports and exercise, spirituality, and psychology.

✔ **Home living:** Covers books on home building, home repair and decorating, gardening, crafts, and antiques.

✔ **Science and nature:** Includes books on serious scientific topics and environmental issues, and may include books on animals and guides for pet owners.

✔ **Visual and performing arts:** Includes books on art, artists, art technique, photography, music and musicians, dance, film, and television.

Children's books

Children's books are often a large category in general bookstores, and they're also a common specialization among independent bookshops. The key to selling children's books is knowledge and passion for the category.

If you're thinking that selling children's books is just a matter of ordering a bunch of classics, shelving them, and waiting for grandparents with fat wallets to come through the door, you're bound to be discouraged by reality. Truth be told, buyers of children's books at general bookstores are usually adults who need guidance as to what books are appropriate for their children, grandchildren, nieces and nephews, friends' kids, and so on. They come to you for that information. If you're not interested in rereading classics and reading new books for kids, then think ahead. You need either to give up the idea of selling children's books as a part of your mix or to hire a manager and one or two other employees who are passionate about the category to work the section whenever your store is open for business.

Children's booksellers have a passion for children's books and find a way — often by making extensive use of sidelines (see the "Making the Most of Sidelines" section, later in this chapter) — to make their bookshops profitable. Keep in mind that children's bookshops have a unique — and somewhat disconcerting — quality in that the core customers disappear every ten years or so (well, they grow up, but it amounts to the same thing). Sure, parents continue to bring younger siblings to the store, and each generation of kids may become parents (and parents may become grandparents). So, you don't exactly start from scratch, but the reality is that you can't count on loyal customers buying children's books coming back to your store, year in and year out, for the rest of their lives.

Another unique facet of children's books is that every other guy on the street thinks he can write them, so you often have to be more selective in your book buying (see Chapter 5) than you may with other categories.

Some children's bookshops carry just a few adult products, such as one or two display tables of bestselling fiction, plus magazines and newspapers set up near couches or library tables. Parents get a chance to peruse books while their kids shop the store.

Computer and technology books

Computer books and *technology books* are the same thing: books that help your customers better understand computer hardware, computer software, the Internet, company intranets, servers, programming languages, and the like. Unless you're in a specialized category or two (such as children's books or travel books), chances are that you can sell some technology books. A suburban market that's not in a high-tech area of the country may not seem suited to technology books, but think about it: Just about everybody uses computers, and just about everyone struggles with theirs at some point.

If you're thinking of carrying a limited number of technology books, consider limiting this category to books about particular software, especially the so-called *desktop applications,* such as Word, Excel, PowerPoint, and Access (and other word-processing, spreadsheet, presentation, and database software). Add to that some Internet titles — books ranging from basics about how to get on the Web to specifics about researching genealogy online or starting an e-Bay business — and you have yourself a small but effective technology category.

Displaying branded products

You can display branded products in two ways: In a branded display pack (one that you can likely get for free from the publisher, if your order is large enough) or in the individual sections to which they relate.

Publishers, of course, want you to display branded books in one place to strengthen the brand and enable customers to browse the brand without having a particular topic in mind. Customers may discover, for example, that they thoroughly enjoy reading some yellow-and-black branded books and wouldn't mind reading more! By grouping this brand together, customers can make a beeline for that display and find more to read.

However, many booksellers prefer placing branded books in their individual categories. While the brand brings an established group of core customers and plenty of instant recognition, most booksellers still buy branded books for their values as individual titles, not for the brand. For this reason, the books are shelved in sections and compete with all other books on that topic. Customers who are looking for a book in a particular category may choose the branded product simply because it stands out among other books within the category; they also may select the branded product on its own merit.

Business books, professional reference books, and textbooks

Most business books stocked by bookstores are *trade* books (available to the book trade and sold to bookstores at standard or trade discounts). But some booksellers are successful stocking more specialized titles known as *professional reference (pro-ref)* books (books often geared to a specific business or profession, printed in smaller quantities and generally offered at a lower discount to booksellers). Some *pro-ref* books are enormous and expensive products — upwards of $100 per title — that target engineers, architects, actuaries, chefs, attorneys, and other professionals. A great market for these types of books is your local government, which may use them for everyday reference at employees' desks, in agency libraries, or in training. See Chapter 9 for tips on tapping this institutional market.

Building a business with books for builders

Back in 1981, Sally and George Kiskaddon, who had been employed in the California real estate industry when it went belly-up, began to notice a lack of books for builders and subcontractors. They were intrigued, however, by the number and the quality of art and architecture bookstores that were thriving. An idea began to emerge: What if they combined architecture and building, and created a bookstore to serve both niches?

What if, indeed! Sally and George's store, Builder's Booksource in San Francisco, is a fine example of a successful specialized bookstore. If you're thinking of running your own specialized store, take a look at some of the decisions the Kiskaddons made about their bookshop's specialty:

✔ **Take on a specialty you're passionate about.** No, Sally and George aren't wild necessarily about plumbing, but they do love architecture, houses, building, remodeling, and many individual aspects of the building process.

✔ **Make sure that your customers understand exactly what your bookstore is about.** Yes, by calling the store "Builder's Booksource," the Kiskaddons didn't have to invest time in people who came in looking for cookbooks or travel guides.

✔ **Don't veer from your specialty.** True. The Kiskaddons frequently review the categories in their store to see which ones they need to expand or contract (see the "Keeping an Eye on Your Categories" section later in this chapter for more), but they wouldn't dream of adding a small section on yoga books, for example.

✔ **Make sure your sidelines fit your specialty.** George and Sally carry few sidelines, but each year they stock chocolate toolsets and toolboxes that are always a huge hit. They also carry architecturally themed calendars and note cards, fold-out cards that turn into houses, giant pencils, and so on.

Your customers may clamor for moderately sized, moderately priced books on managing employees, business planning, negotiating, marketing, publicity planning, business communications, entrepreneurship, and so on. Many of these books will be available as trade books, with your usual discount. If your customer base consists of business professionals — either employed by a corporation or self-employed — keep your eye out for appropriate pro-ref titles that you can add to your mix. Even though the discounts are lower, the prices are usually higher, and the presence of some pro-ref titles may convince a local business to make you its book source.

Textbooks are another matter altogether. Because textbook discounts are even slimmer than the discounts on professional reference books, a bookstore that sells textbooks must rely on a high volume of sales. Traditionally, general bookshops don't sell textbooks unless a college in the area isn't adequately serving students' needs. Occasionally, you may be able to fill a need for textbooks geared toward Internet-based courses, adult education classes, or church study groups.

University and small press books

Although few stores can successfully specialize in books from university presses and other small presses (bookstores in college towns are a possible exception), most independent booksellers do carry some university and small press titles.

U Press 101

Traditionally, university (U) presses have been subsidized by their parent institutions, allowing them more freedom to publish books that wouldn't be considered profitable by their counterparts in trade publishing.

More and more, however, U presses are treated as independent subsidiaries, expected to "make it" on their own. Therefore, many university presses publish more trade books, which is a good thing for booksellers and for authors who may not be able to make the numbers at a large trade publisher.

U presses also publish academic titles, which are usually offered at a *short discount* (another way of saying small discount) to booksellers. Because discounts are as low as 20 percent and the topics are more rarified, you probably won't stock these titles unless your store is in the heart of an academic market. If your store can stock academic titles, you need to network with professors and graduate students to find out what's hot and what's not. Because they're written by professors who are on the cutting edge of their disciplines, academic books can be as subject to the whims of intellectual trends and fashion.

In fact, many bookshops like to support small presses, which are equivalent to independent booksellers on the publishing side of the book biz. University presses and other small presses tend to publish titles that are considered successful when they sell 5,000 or 10,000 copies, a number that would disappoint most large publishers. However, just as you may carry individual titles that don't sell extraordinarily well but are important books to have on your shelves, independent presses can publish titles that are outside of mainstream thinking or considered too "academic" for larger publishers when sales expectations aren't so high.

Travel books and foreign-language books

One of the best features of travel books is that they work in so many different types of bookstores. Suppose, for example, that your bookstore is located in a beautiful tourist area where no one ever leaves home. Can't sell travel books? Sure you can — to all the tourists who visit the town and want to explore the area with the help of a guidebook.

Live in a bleak, dreary, or especially hot or cold area? Customers in your town probably look forward to their out-of-town vacations the way that someone walking across the desert looks forward to a dribble of water. Stock a wide variety of travel books for both easy getaways and exotic trips.

One downside to travel books is that many publishers plan for new editions each year. Customers like this because they're getting the most up-to-date information about prices, phone numbers, and Web sites. You don't want to end up with a lot of returns, however, so order based on last year's sales and check when the new editions are coming out before you place reorders (see Chapter 6). This planned obsolescence is also a reason why selling used travel books isn't usually a good idea (see the "Used books" section, later in this chapter).

Deciding whether to stock foreign-language books is a tough call, and most independent bookstores have only a small selection, if any. Basic language books that teach or help readers brush up on a language may sell well in your area, as may language books that are used for reference while traveling. If a large population in your area regards English as a second language, then books on English as a foreign language and books in the native tongue may succeed. In college towns, all manner of foreign-language books often sell well.

Local books

Local books come in two categories:

- ✔ **Local interest books about your area:** Local interest books usually sell especially well in tourist destinations, because tourists want a reminder of their terrific time in your town. But booksellers in all markets find that any new book about that city or town is of interest to residents, too.

- ✔ **Books on any subject by local authors who live nearby:** Books by local authors can have a tremendous draw, especially in a smaller town, because customers tend to support one of their own. Consider stocking local fiction, essays, poetry, general reference — in short, books by any local author who may have a following among your customers.

Just because an author is local doesn't mean that your customers are going to buy his or her books. Although you want to support your local authors, just as they support your shop, don't choose a book by a local author that you would never order if the author lived 3,000 miles away. Make sure that the book is the type of book you carry and is of the quality your customers expect.

Jonathan Rand's series, *Michigan Chillers,* is an example of local books that have exceeded expectations among independent booksellers and have grown to include a national market. Rand, a Michigan native, started these books for kids in various cities around Michigan (the book jacket points out the geographic area of Michigan in which the mystery takes place), and they've been wildly popular in the state. More recently, however, when he met kids from out of state, they asked for books from their home towns, so Rand's publisher expanded the series, calling it *American Chillers.* Now the Michigan booksellers who've been carrying his books not only have a strong local writer to support, but an emerging national one, too.

Used books

Used books — already-read books that are purchased from customers, obtained from estate sales, or selected by free-lance used-book scouts — are another category you may already carry or plan to add in the future. (See Chapter 5 for ways to find high-quality used books.) Used books can be a tremendous boon to booksellers because of the high *margins* (selling price minus purchase price) they inspire. Although a new book may sell for $16 and cost $9.60 (a 40 percent discount), a used book may sell for $5 and cost $1 (an 80 percent discount). Another advantage to selling used books is that you can commit fewer dollars to inventory and have a larger selection of books. (Keep in mind, however, that in this example, the new book makes $6.40 while the used makes $4, and both may require effort in buying, stocking, and selling the title.) Customers tend not to be confused by the integration of new and used books, because the used books are usually labeled and are offered at a far lower price. This system also makes deciding on which used books to buy even easier: You buy only the categories of used books that you also buy new.

Of course, some booksellers also separate used books into one area, sometimes even with a separate entrance to clearly delineate the two types of books offered.

Be wary of used books that quickly lose their luster, such as annually revised travel guides, technology books for software or programming languages that have been revised, business reference books for practices that are no longer in vogue, encyclopedias, biographies of living people who have gotten (or may still get) into trouble, geography books for areas in political turmoil, and social/political commentary that is no longer relevant. For many stores, mass market titles don't sell well in used editions, in part because they get so beat up after a single reading.

Used books are one area in which Amazon.com is less of a competitor and more of a customer! When Amazon doesn't carry a particular title, Web surfers have the chance to order the book used, often directly from the inventories of small, independent bookstores. If you're selling used books, contact Amazon to have your inventory listed as a link on their site.

Remainders

Overstocks, also called *remainders* or *hurts,* are titles that publishers want to clear out of their warehouses. Some remainders are titles that booksellers have returned to publishers; others may be books that were over-printed and never shipped. You can buy remainders from sales reps, who may specialize in remaindered books or who represent both new and remaindered books. These reps also may represent books from one publisher or many. You can find remaindered books at shows, including CIROBE and BEA, and through lists available via fax, e-mail, and the Internet. See Chapter 5 for more details.

Regardless of where you purchase remainders, you'll get a tremendous discount on the titles — sometimes as much as 80 or 90 percent, which means that you can sell them at less than half of the original retail price and even make a better profit than you did when you sold the book at full price. Use remainders as a draw to get people into your store, especially when placed as sidewalk sales or as discount tables near the store's entrance. You can also integrate remainders with your new books, placing them side-by-side on your shelves. Keep in mind, however, that you can't return remainders, and you don't want to mistake them for a full-priced book when a customer brings one back. If remainders aren't already marked when they arrive, consider marking them with a small black line on the bottom edge of the book's pages. Also, remainders sometimes look a little tattered, because they get jostled during the return process or dusty sitting on a warehouse shelf.

When buying remainders, a good bet is to match your frontlist buying (see Chapter 5); that is, stick to the same categories as you do for new books. Matching your frontlist buying is especially easy if you shelve new and remaindered books together. In addition, you may identify some categories that you can't sell at full price, but that do well with remainders: art books and coffee table books, for example.

Keeping an Eye on Your Categories

The categories you choose to include in your store are simply the proper choices for your store *today*. Trends, innovations, changes in the population around your store — heck, even your own changing interests and passions — mean that the categories you stock are always in flux. Some of the categories you stock today will not be categories you carry in ten years — or even in two years. If you decide on certain categories and staunchly refuse to change them or you refuse to change the layout of your store so as not to upset customers, you're likely to lose business as customers go looking for hot new categories/atmosphere elsewhere. (To look for these trends, check out *Publisher's Weekly's* trend reports that come out every month or two.)

Each month, analyze how every category you carry is performing (that is, how well books in each section have sold) and from that analysis, proceed as described in the following sections.

Grow the category

If books in a category are selling well — expand the category in one of two ways:

✓ **Carry a greater number of titles in that category.** If you're successfully selling a single title on ferrets, you may be able to give customers a greater choice (and increase sales) by offering a second title.

✓ **Carry more copies of the particular titles that you frequently run out of.** Instead of stocking just one or two copies of a title because you're short on space for a category, expand the space for this category (usually by reducing the size of another — see the following section) and carry enough to *face out* the book (show its front cover rather than its spine) on the shelf.

You can also grow a category not just by expanding it in general but by expanding it into even better-defined subcategories. Shaman Drum bookshop in Ann Arbor, Michigan, carries at least a dozen subcategories within the larger category of Buddhism. Books on Buddhism sell extremely well at this store that's located right in the center of the University of Michigan, a school that offers one of the few Ph.D. programs in Buddhism in the country. Contrast this store with one in, say, Salt Lake City, which may sell a lot of books about religion and have a specific category on the Mormon faith, but may never have a customer base that's interested in regularly buying books on Eastern religions.

The categories in the chain superstores are mostly set at the corporate level and reflect national interests, not regional ones. One major benefit that an independent bookstore has over a chain superstore is that the local bookstore can reflect local tastes and preferences. A corporate superstore in Anchorage may carry a category called "winter sports," while an independent bookseller in that same town may have categories of snowmobiling, snowshoeing, cross country skiing, ice skating, speedskating, hockey, tobogganing, snowboarding, downhill skiing, ice fishing, dog sledding, and *skijoring* (cross-country skiing while being pulled by a large dog!) — each with as much or more depth as the one category in the superstore. Take a look at the categories in your closest corporate superstore and see whether your community can support more depth in particular categories.

Shrink the category

If you find that books do sell in a particular category, but sell infrequently, now may be the time to cut down the number of titles you carry in that category. If you've given the category your best shot, return any book that hasn't sold in several months (see Chapter 6) and keep only those titles that you're reordering with some frequency.

One way to shrink a category but still make it look large and varied is to combine one category with another (similar) one. For example, if cookbooks are a large category for you but you find that the subcategories of Japanese cooking and Korean cooking are shrinking, consider combining the two into Asian cooking. Besides, by combining two or more categories, you may be able to expand another category.

Eliminate the category

Eliminating a category may seem like sacrilege, but doing so is both legal and moral. If a category (such as a cutting-edge pop culture section in a suburban bedroom community, or a wilderness sports section in a large city) just doesn't sell at all in your store after tracking it for a few months, pack up the books in the section, return them to the publishers (see Chapter 6), and don't order more.

If a category makes sense for your store — a mountain-climbing category in Denver or a ranching section in Boise — make sure that you're giving that category every possible opportunity for success. Before you eliminate it, be sure that the category is positioned in an area that visitors are likely to notice and spend time in, make sure that the signs for the area are large and readable, and double-check that the section is appealing in its displays and arrangement of shelved books (see Chapter 7).

A category doesn't have to work geographically to work. A rock-climbing book may become popular in Kansas City if a new climbing wall goes up in a city park; a section on Asian cooking may sell well in a city with only a small Asian-American population if a popular TV show highlights Asian-American cuisine. Don't stereotype your customers and write off a category before you've tried it. Find out about your customers' interests (refer to Chapter 3) and stock categories they say they want, not just the ones you think are "appropriate" based on gender, ethnicity, geography, age, and so on.

Also, keep in mind that some books are seasonal (dieting books in January, books about love around Valentine's Day, outdoor grilling books in summer, and so on), so they should be reduced or eliminated in the off-season and brought back to life in-season.

Making the Most of Sidelines

Sidelines are non-book products that you sell in your store, either in their own separate displays or integrated with books. Sidelines are often gift items that don't necessarily tie-in to books but do allow for one-stop shopping by the customer.

You can price sidelines however you want, because the price isn't marked on the package. (Of course, every item must be individually priced with pricing guns — and that's a lot of work!)

You have no return privileges with sidelines, which means that everything you buy is purchased outright. To make sure you don't get stuck with inventory you can't sell, take the following precautions:

✔ Add together your wholesale price plus the freight, and then at least double that amount (called *keystoning*) to arrive at your retail price. In your pricing, be sure to account for future markdowns for some of the products.

✔ Keep sidelines affordable. When the price point gets too high, they just don't sell. Look for affordable pieces of art that are under $50. If you want to sell more expensive items, sell lamps, tables, stained glass, and framed art that can enhance the beauty of your store as it's displayed.

✔ Keep your sidelines trendy, interesting, and exciting. What worked a year ago may not work this year.

✔ Order in small quantities and reorder frequently (you're passing along the freight cost to customers, so reordering frequently won't hurt you). Don't get so excited about a sideline that you over-order. If the minimum required order is too high (say, $250 in candles), look for another company that will work with you.

Space is the biggest challenge when carrying sidelines. You just never have enough space to display your sidelines effectively. However, sidelines can make a store far more attractive and can help the store better reflect the owners' tastes and the store's mission (refer to Chapter 2). For most bookshops, though, books remain at least 70 to 75 percent of the store's sales.

Bookstores commonly carry any or all of the following sidelines:

✔ Audio books.

✔ Blank journals: You can create some displays with blank journals, a beautiful pen, and writing or journaling books.

✔ Book lights, bookmarks, bookends, and pens.

✔ Calendars, date books, and organizers.

✔ Cards and stationery: You can carry even a dozen card lines. Try to get a *card tower,* which is made of wood and acrylic, not wire, so that each pocket can hold cards of all shapes — and lots of them.

- Children's bath products, such as body crayons, Tub Tints, floating bath toys, plastic bath books, washcloths and towels.

- Chopsticks, ceramic rest for chopsticks, sushi-related products.

- Clothing accessories, such as purses and scarves.

- Coasters, trivets, napkins, placemats.

- DVDs and videos.

- European soaps, lotions, massage oils, and bath products. These products can be paired with mind-body-spirit books in displays. Watch sales of these sorts of products very closely and always start with small quantities (make the minimum order initially).

- Family games.

- Gift wrap and gift bags.

- Incense and candles.

- Jewelry (funky earrings, necklaces).

- Jigsaw puzzles, educational toys and games (especially in the children's department).

- Magnetic poetry.

- Magnifiers and eyewear.

- Mobiles that hang from the ceiling.

- Music CDs: If you're going to sell music, keep in mind that the discount is even less than with books. However, you can do a tremendous amount of volume in a small space. Hire one or two people who are knowledgeable about music, and if at all possible, include listening stations, which customers eat up.

- Office supplies.

- Photo albums.

- Plush toys (teddy bears and the like) and puppets: Be sure to keep these under control, because they seem to multiply at night!

- Pottery, lamps, and small sculptures.

- Small rugs.

- Tea pots, tea sets, and local gourmet tea.

- Unframed prints (one print bin with about 100 prints that range from $12 to $20); poster frames.

- Wind chimes.

- Yoga mats, aromatherapy eye pillows.

- Zen gardens (with rake, sand, and rocks) and meditation pillows.

Keep plenty of boxes and bubble wrap at the checkout counter so that breakable sidelines get home safely.

Does the preceding list seem like too much to possibly contemplate? Although several items on the list are items that nearly every bookshop carries, more than half came from Changing Hands bookstore in Tempe, Arizona, which carries nearly every one of these items in the store. Okay, Changing Hands is housed in a former Walgreen's location with 10,000 square feet of selling space, so you may have to adjust this list down a bit to fit your situation, but this list helps you see what's possible.

Selling news: Magazines and newspapers

Some stores sell magazines and newspapers in addition to books and other sidelines; other booksellers avoid them like the plague. Magazine price-points are low, discounts are horrible (usually 20 percent) and keeping up with the weekly deliveries and returns takes you or one of your staff members the better part of a full day (or even more). Newspapers are a little less time-consuming, but they're rather smelly and messy — and the unsold Sunday editions take up space in your back room.

The main reason to consider selling news is to increase traffic in your store. A customer who may not think she needs a book may come in to pick up a magazine or a daily paper, creating the habit of shopping at your store. If you provide a pleasant experience and a good selection, you may win yourself a book customer. Place your top sellers and your impulse items between your magazine rack and your cash register to jump-start add-on sales.

Chapter 5

Buy the Book: Where to Find Books and Other Products

· ·

In This Chapter

▶ Going to the source: buying books directly from publishers

▶ Using an effective middle man: buying from wholesalers

▶ Finding sources for used books

▶ Getting into the remainder business

▶ Finding complementary sidelines for your bookshop

· ·

*W*hether you're ordering *frontlist* titles months in advance of their publication, reordering *backlist* books, looking for sources of used and remaindered books, or enhancing the look and convenience of your bookshop (in addition to enhancing your margins) with sidelines, this chapter shows you where to go and whom to contact. (For a definition of italicized terms, see the sidebar, "Frontlist and midlist and backlist, oh my!")

Margins refer to the amount of money you have left when you subtract your purchase price and freight costs from the selling price that your customers pay. Margins on books from wholesalers and some university and small presses are among the smallest of the products you sell; margins on books ordered directly from publishers are usually a little higher than what wholesalers offer; margins on used books, remainders, and sidelines are quite high when compared to publisher and wholesaler book margins.

Frontlist Buying: Ordering from Publishers

Frontlist buying is a bit like gambling: You place an order for a particular book and when it finally gets into customers' hands several months later, you hope it's a book your customers enjoy spending time with. This section helps you improve those Las Vegas odds.

Frontlist and midlist and backlist, oh my!

If some of the words in this chapter sound like Greek to you, check out the following bookshop buzzwords:

- ✔ *Frontlist* titles are new titles from publishers. Publishers promote frontlist titles through catalogs, which they usually produce two to three times per year. Each catalog represents a publishing season (spring, fall, winter). Bookstores usually order frontlist titles several months in advance of their publication date or *BBD* (bound-book date). To know which frontlist titles to order, you review catalogs, meet with sales and telemarketing reps and — of course — rely on your knowledge of your customers' reading preferences.

- ✔ *Midlist* books are frontlist titles that are expected to produce modest sales. In other words, midlist books are not expected to

be bestsellers. A midlist title may be a novel from a new author or a more literary work that won't be likely to hit the charts.

- ✔ *Sleepers* are midlist books that *break out* (produce sales that exceed the publisher's expectations). Often, sleepers break out because they're read by independent booksellers who *hand-sell* them, actually putting the book into the hands of their customers, with a strong and personal recommendation. (See Chapter 9 for details.)

- ✔ *Backlist* includes all of the books you've ordered in the past. These books have been placed on your shelves, you've sold them to customers, and you now need to order them again. Backlist books are the reliable sellers you want to keep in stock at all times.

Frontlist buying requires four key components:

✔ Knowing what new titles are coming out and when they'll arrive.

✔ Seeing the book's cover, discussing the planned print run, and reviewing marketing plans for every potential title.

✔ Reviewing sales for books on the same topic (or by a repeat author) to see how well you've sold similar titles.

✔ Determining how your customers will respond to each title.

Before you order, know your store's categories (refer to Chapter 4), so that you know what sells in your store. Order based on your knowledge of the store and your customers. Visualize your store as you order: Decide as best you can, when placing every order, where that merchandise is going to go when it arrives.

In order to know how much of a frontlist book to order, keep a mental image of your store — where you have which categories, what the space looks like, and where each fixture is located. Also keep in mind the sales patterns of those sections and the interests and needs of your customers. How much you order of each title depends on how many you think you can sell within a given period of time. The factors that may influence your sales are the size of your shop and available display space, your knowledge of your customers' buying patterns, past sales of a particular author, and your personal reaction to the titles that are presented to you.

✔ If you feel strongly about a title and can envision certain customers snapping it up, order enough copies to feature the book in some way. Depending on the size and layout of your store, this book display could mean that you create stacks on your front table, showcase the book in your new title area, or face it out within a section.

Some stores use bestsellers or other big titles as *loss leaders* to bring customers into the store and to reinforce to customers that they can get bestselling titles at a competitive price. Using a book as a loss leader means you may lose money on it. Although this tactic used to be limited to chain bookselling, more and more independent stores choose to discount a limited and carefully selected group of titles to change customers' perception that small, local stores charge more.

✔ Order one or two copies of a book you're less sure about or can't imagine particular customers selecting. If the book sells well, quickly order more (see the "Ordering from Wholesalers" section, later in this chapter).

✔ If you need to fill an order with one last book, consider taking a chance with one copy of a title and seeing how it sells.

If you're unsure of how many copies to order, look at the appeal of the cover or jacket. Is this book going to attract attention, stand out in a crowded sea of books? Is the book the type that you sell well? If so, order enough copies to stack on a feature table or to face-out on a shelf. If not, order just one or two.

Rather than relying on industry publications (see Chapter 6) for frontlist buying, use publisher's catalogs. Two or three times per year, publishers produce catalogs for their upcoming frontlist titles — books that will be published three to six months down the road. Catalogs describe the book in words, give specs (like the publication date, size, price, and ISBN), display the book's cover, give an author's bio (including whether the author lives in your geographic area), and explain the marketing plan (the promotional budget, the radio/TV/print publicity, print runs, and so on).

To place a frontlist order based on what you've seen in catalogs, you work either with a sales representative or a telemarketing rep.

Working with sales reps

Before placing frontlist orders, some booksellers meet with *publishers' representatives* (or sales reps) for each major publishing company. These reps service a geographic area and travel from bookshop to bookshop, calling on book buyers (often the owners). Reps discuss further what's in catalogs, spending between 30 seconds and two minutes discussing each potential frontlist title. Your rep may also be able to get you advance copies of books (see Chapter 9 for details).

Try to develop a relationship with your rep, treating him or her as part of your bookselling team. If you rely on your rep's visits to get the information you need about each title, you can make better buying judgments. Even if you're new to bookselling or your rep has taken over for someone you'd worked with for years, in just one or two appointments, you can get to know each other and start to build a mutually respectful relationship.

Reps know that being honest pays off in the long run. If a rep pushes books that are inappropriate for your market and that you can't sell, you'll be less inclined to pay attention to that rep's claims in the future.

Going through telemarketing reps

Sales reps cover large territories and, whether they want to or not, they can never visit all of the stores in the territory. (Yes, publishers could make their territories smaller, but then they'd have to hire more reps, which would cut into their profits.) To extend their reach, publishers set up a telephone sales department.

If your store is one that's not often on the map of sales reps or if you aren't available the day a rep sets up appointments in your neck of the woods, you can go through *telemarketing reps* who call you and present information over the phone. These reps can send catalogs and arrange to review the publishers' list with you by telephone.

Telephone visits can be valuable. Telemarketing reps are well trained: They attend sales conferences just as traveling sales reps do, and they know their publisher's list. Because telephone reps work in an office environment, they're in a better position to follow up quickly on potential co-op money (see the following section) or other administrative tasks that can be more challenging for reps who are always on the road.

To make phone visits productive, treat the calls the same way you would an in-person sales call. Make an appointment, review the list in advance, set aside the time to meet in a quiet place, have your catalogs ready, and keep a computer nearby. Although many buyers wish they could meet with a rep in person (especially buyers from stores who used to qualify for a rep visit, but no longer do), they do find that they can develop an enjoyable working relationship with their reps at a distance.

Making a co-operative effort

Publishers sometimes offer *co-op money* (short for cooperative advertising or promotions in which publishers and booksellers share the costs) to help promote their books. Some co-op dollars come with strings attached (for example, you must spend the money on newspaper ads, or you get the money only if you fill an endcap display with certain titles from the publisher). Other co-op dollars, however, are more fluid: You're given a piece of a publicity pie, and you can spend that money any way you choose. The money given is usually a percentage of your order for one title or for your entire order in one season; it may also be based on the previous year's sales with that publisher.

If co-op money isn't mentioned by your sales rep, pitch an idea to him or her, even if the publisher rarely offers co-op money. Some common ideas for getting co-op money include the following:

- ✔ Feature the book prominently in the store's newsletter or on your Web site.

- ✔ Run a radio or newspaper ad for a title, perhaps in conjunction with other booksellers in your area.

- ✔ Bring in an author for a book-signing or other event. Some publishers offer even more than their usual co-op amounts for author events. The more imaginative these events — ones that customers will excitedly put on their calendars — the more co-op money you're likely to get. Co-op money can pay for food and decorations, too.

- ✔ Hold a book fair or literary festival that highlights a particular book or series.

- ✔ Sponsor a writing contest that relates to a particular book or publisher at your local school or library.

- ✔ Offer a workshop or seminar related to the book's topic.

- ✔ Underwrite a PBS (public television) or NPR (public radio) show with a mention of the book. If this promotion costs too much for your budget, consider underwriting a movie opening, film series, or play at your local theater, or sponsoring your local symphony, opera company, or ballet company.

After the promotion, be sure to keep copies of how you spent every cent of your co-op money — the publisher will need that information for its records.

Making the most of publisher's promotions

Publishers sometimes offer promotional tools — some of which you can pass on to customers — for certain products. For example, when Penguin relaunched the *Penguin Classics,* they offered totebags for booksellers to give away free with a purchase. Other examples include Betty Crocker cake mixes given away for free to promote Betty Crocker Cookbooks and Frommer's luggage tags that are displayed with Frommer's travel guides. All of these types of publisher's promotions are offered free to you by publishers and can definitely help sell books.

Publishers may also offer a free, often attractive, and brightly colored *display pack* (also called floor displays or dumps) in which you can display books. You may also be offered a discount or free freight for purchasing a particular product at a certain level.

The challenge with publisher's promotions is that the titles still have to be appropriate for your store. Don't let promotional tools sway you into buying a product that just won't work for you. If you buy a title at a great discount and you get free freight, an attractive display pack, and some free giveaways — but you can't sell the book in your store, you've just wasted time and money. Although you can always return the books later, you have to pay freight to return them, and your buying money is tied up in publishers' credits.

Many booksellers take advantage of promotions only if they were going to order the book anyway or if they're very close to the level of orders needed. So, if you up your order by one or two books and get all sorts of free tools for promoting the book, that's terrific. But if you have to double or triple your order in order to take advantage of publisher's promotions, pass on the deal.

Ordering from Wholesalers

When you've sold frontlist copies of books and are now restocking your shelves with that same title again, you have two options: ordering from publishers or ordering from wholesalers. See Chapter 6 for all sort of tips and tricks for knowing which books to reorder and how often to order them.

Wholesalers (also called *distributors* or *jobbers*) are book middlemen: They buy books in large quantities from publishers, store them in warehouses around the country, and resell them to bookstores. The biggest wholesalers are Baker & Taylor, Bookazine, Ingram, and Koen.

For backlist titles, ordering from wholesalers offers some of the following advantages over buying directly from publishers:

- ✔ **Orders arrive fast.** When a bookseller orders from a wholesaler, the order is often shipped that day and arrives the next, although if your store is in a remote area, delivery can take up to three days. Contrast this with most publishers, whose orders arrive in five to ten business days.

- ✔ **You can keep your inventory low.** Because just about any book is only one day away, you can keep your inventory levels low and reorder daily, as most booksellers do.

  You can order conservatively on frontlist titles from the publisher, and then reorder quickly from a wholesaler.

- ✔ **Most wholesalers often offer an early-payment discount.** You may find that you can juggle your finances to take advantage of those discounts.

- ✔ **Wholesalers sometimes carry backlist titles that publishers don't.** Strange as this may sound, many booksellers find that they can get backlist titles from wholesalers that just aren't available from publishers. This situation occurs because the publisher has sold out of all its copies and hasn't yet reprinted. Meanwhile, the wholesaler still has some of that last printing on hand for you to order.

- ✔ **You can get lots of books from different publishers in one shipment.** One shipment is easier to track than eight or ten, so wholesalers streamline your receiving process (see Chapter 6 for more on receiving inventory).

✔ **Freight is almost always free.** More and more, freight is also free when ordering directly from the big publishing houses, but smaller publishers and university presses often do charge freight. Given the hefty weight of hardcover books, this cost can add up.

But buying from wholesalers has a downside, right? Unfortunately, yes. Here's the scoop:

✔ **Discounts are lower.** Many publishers offer a discount of 43 to 46 percent off the list price, while wholesalers generally offer a 40 to 42 percent discount, which makes for smaller margins. However, if you order a certain amount of products and take advantage of wholesalers' early-payment discounts, you may be able to achieve a slightly higher average discount from wholesalers.

Occasionally, discounts are even smaller — as low as 20 percent — for books from small presses or university presses.

✔ **More co-op money is usually available by ordering directly from publishers.** You can accrue co-op dollars from publishers for orders placed through wholesalers, but the process is a little more complicated — and you usually get a smaller piece of the co-op pie. For more information on co-op dollars, see the "Making a co-operative effort" section earlier in this chapter.

✔ **Wholesalers don't carry certain titles.** Wholesalers place an emphasis on titles that they can turn around quickly. They may not carry slower-moving books, especially titles from university presses or small and regional publishers.

✔ **If a publisher messes up an order, you can have your rep on the phone within the hour.** If a wholesaler makes a mistake on your order, on the other hand, getting a quick correction can be more difficult to do. Some booksellers find this not to be true, however.

✔ **The wholesaler may charge a restocking fee for returns.** Or, they may place a limit on how much of what you order in a given year can be returned (typically 10 percent). Most publishers don't impose a fee on returns or limit your returns. See Chapter 6 for more on returns.

Getting an overview of the book publishing biz

Each publisher manages book projects uniquely, but most follow a process that somewhat resembles the following:

1. **An author, agent, or publishing house identifies a market for a particular book title.**

   The title may still be in the idea stage, as is often the case with nonfiction titles and series books, or it may be a submitted manuscript.

   If the publishing house is identifying the market, the process may be as simple as determining which similar titles are in circulation and how sales of those book have fared. This process may also be far more exhaustive, using sales conferences to gauge how sales reps feel about their ability to promote the title or bringing in focus groups to determine consumer reaction to a particular title.

2. **An editor or publishing team acquires the title.**

   If the title is still only an idea, acquiring the title means finding an appropriate author; agreeing with that author to an advance, royalites, and due dates for the manuscript; and signing a contract. An *acquiring editor,* also called an *acquisitions editor,* usually takes care of this process.

If the title was suggested by a particular author in the form of a proposal and sample text, a publishing review board often meets to discuss the proposal and give it (and the author) a thumbs up or thumbs down. The acquiring editor then tries to come to terms with the author (advance, royalties, due dates) and, if necessary, find a co-author to assist the author.

If the title was submitted as a complete manuscript, a review board or editor reads the manuscript and makes a decision about whether to publish that title by that author. The editor then tries to come to terms with the author or author team.

3. **Marketing and PR go to work.**

   Creative types design a cover, draft press releases, design and print catalog pages, and so on. When sales reps visit your bookshop, you're seeing the result of the marketing and PR effort.

4. **Various editors work their magic on the manuscript.**

   These editors range from *development editors* (who review the organization of the manuscript and make sure it meets the publisher's vision) to *copyeditors* (who edit the manuscript line by line) to *permissions editors* (who make sure the text legally belongs to the author) to *project editors* (who manage the book process from acquisitions to bound book and may also develop and copyedit the manuscript). Every publisher chooses different names for this team of editors; some have tremendous authority over the book's content, others have no authority at all.

5. **The manuscript is laid out, proofed, printed, and bound.**

Some publishers employ an in-house staff of graphics and page-layout experts; others free-lance part of the process to individuals or production companies.

Books are sometimes printed in-house, but are often sent away to printing houses, which may be as far away as China.

Galleys (or galley proofs), which range from unbound printed pages held together with a rubber band to a bound book with a mock cover, are sometimes available for reviewers and booksellers. Galleys have gone through layout but not through proofreading, printing, and binding.

6. **The bound book arrives in the publisher's warehouse(s) and is shipped to wholesalers and bookshops that have ordered the title.**

Some booksellers handle the pros and cons of wholesalers by ordering conservatively when they place their frontlist orders (directly from publishers, two or three times per year). They then place orders with wholesalers as often as *every day,* quickly reordering any titles that sell rapidly or are special-ordered by customers. (See Chapter 9 for more on special orders.)

Getting Used to Used Books

Used books offer booksellers advantages that new books can't. Because publishers price new books, you don't have the opportunity to determine the price on your own — so you try to make a living selling books at the prices publishers establish. But you do price used books: You can buy used books cheap and mark them up at three or more times your cost. Sometimes, you can mark up a book *way* more than three times, buying it for 25 cents and selling it for $3.99. In this way, margins on used book can be quite profitable.

The downside, of course, is that you can't make returns the way you can with new books, so you have to be savvy about what you buy and in what condition you buy them.

- ✓ Look for used books in good condition, with covers and spines intact.

- ✓ Avoid titles that quickly become dated, such as technology books, social and political commentary, biographies of living persons, and annual travel guides.

- ✓ Avoid encyclopedias, given the availability of online and CD-based encyclopedias that are always up-to-date.

- ✓ Beware of books that are in perfect — perhaps even sealed — condition. They may have been stolen from another bookshop.

If you buy your books from customers, you may be buying books you know you can't sell because you value their business. After all, they're nice people, so you don't want to refuse the book. But, if you're going to succeed at buying an inventory of used books that will sell quickly, you have to find ways to say "no" to books you don't want.

Buying books over the counter from customers is a terrific way to find high-quality used books, especially if you offer credit on your shop's new books in exchange. Beside customers bringing in books over the counter, you can also hire a freelance *scout* who can go out and buy inventory for you. (A scout can be especially useful when you're just starting to sell used books; he or she can procure your opening inventory.) You can frequent estate sales and buy out entire libraries from book lovers, visit swap meets and flea markets, and peruse thrift shops and antique stores. Even Saturday-morning garage sales (also called tag sales and yard sales) can be a good source of used books.

Finding Remainders of the Day

Consider getting into *remainder* business, which is another name for publisher's overstock. When you sell remaindered books, you're selling other booksellers' returns, which you get for a song — so remainders are a terrific way to increase your margins. Remainders look new, although they may be slightly tattered from the return process and may have a black mark on the top or bottom of the spine, which keeps them from being returned in the future for full credit. Refer to Chapter 4 for more on the pros and cons of remainders.

Many categories of remainders sell well. Art books, which are great for the holidays, are often popular as remainders, as are hard-to-find books, such as large-print titles. Fiction (paperback), biography, history, health, children's, and parenting books also tend to sell well as remainders. Be sure, however, to stick to the categories that tend to sell well in your store, matching up your remainders with your frontlist buying. If a book sells out in hardcover and it's available a year later as a remainder, you know it's probably going to sell in your store.

If you think a category will sell well in your store but you can't afford to buy frontlist books for it, consider buying remainders for starters. You may be able to buy a small section, for example, for just $500.

If you're thinking of getting into the remainder business, consider attending CIROBE (Chicago International Remainder and Overstock Book Exposition), a national trade show held each fall. Most remainder companies exhibit at the show (see CIROBE's Web site, www.cirobe.com, for a list of exhibitors); you can touch and feel the books, compare prices, and sometimes negotiate deals on specific titles. Another major trade show for remaindered books is held each spring in Atlanta (visit www.springbookshow.com). Daedalus, www.daedalus-books.com, is a major supplier of literary remainder books.

Some sales reps specialize in remainders or sell remainders in addition to frontlist titles, and they visit much more frequently than frontlist sales reps do, simply because their available inventories also change frequently. Use technology aggressively to keep on top of available remainders. Ask reps to send new book lists by e-mail or fax, and check out Web sites that list remaindered titles. Some remainder companies also have showrooms or warehouses you can visit. Check to see whether a remainder company is headquartered near you.

The key with remainders is that quantities are always limited. The sooner you know that a company has purchased a title, the sooner you can take some books off its hands and put them into the hands of your customers.

Before you send back returns, make sure you won't do better selling them as remainders. Although most booksellers return their overstocks and then buy remainders, a few have found that they can sell the books for half-price, rather than return them. They often do just as well as they would with returns, after figuring in the cost of freight and any penalties that wholesalers may charge. Generally, paperbacks will sell for half-price, but hard covers won't, so hard covers are usually returned. Timely items, such as last year's travel paperbacks, also can't be sold for half-price.

Promotional books (sometimes called *bargain books*) are different from remainders. Promotional books are usually reprints of expensive books that are beyond copyright (or the copyright was available cheaply) that are printed on thinner paper than the original books were. Some promotional books are low-priced originals. (Think of the stacks of picture books of dogs and cats you see at many chain outlets.) If the topic is right for your market, you may sell a promotional title well, but most booksellers do better with remainders.

Choosing Up Sidelines

Sidelines can be terrific complements to the books you sell, and because you can keystone sidelines (sell them for at least twice what you paid for them), sidelines improve your margins substantially. Refer to Chapter 4 for a complete listing of the sidelines commonly carried by bookstores.

To find sidelines for your store, start by shopping around at museum gift stores, card shops, gift shops, and your other favorite stores, both in your geographic area and when you travel. When you see something you would buy for yourself that seems appropriate for the store, write down the name of the product and the manufacturer — and also check for a Web site, if one is listed on the packaging. Use the Internet to track down the manufacturer, either by typing in the Web address or by searching on Google or some other search engine. After you locate the company, look for an e-mail address so that you can make contact and get the name of a sales rep, who will visit your store just as a publisher's sales rep does (see the "Working with sales reps" section, earlier in this chapter).

In addition, try to go to at least two gift shows per year, where manufacturers and sales reps put their products on display for you to see and touch. George Little Company (www.glm-shows.com) manages many gift shows around the country. Pro-Mark, Inc. (www.thegiftshows.com) also operates several gift shows around the country. Although you do have to pay for transportation and hotel, the shows are free if you bring your store business card or letterhead. To save on travel costs, look for a show near your hometown: Type **gift shows,** followed by the name of your state or a large city near you, in any Internet search engine.

Some shows specialize in certain products, such as stationery or textiles. Keep in mind, too, that different areas of the country tend to sell different types of products, so a gift show in L.A. may have more New Age or Asian products than a show in New York or Florida does.

When deciding what products to purchase, choose those products that complement your book categories and base your buying decisions on what you know will sell. Buy what you personally like, too: Chances are, if you think a product is attractive, useful, or appropriate for gift-giving, so will your customers. Trust your own tastes. (Of course, you'll make mistakes, which will go on the sale table six months from now. Price your products with the knowledge that you'll make a few errors. Refer to Chapter 4 for details.)

Most sidelines are nonreturnable. If you goof up, you'll have to mark them down and possibly throw them out. As distasteful as this may sound, you'll have better sales overall if you constantly weed out what isn't selling and replace it with fresh merchandise. Trends and tastes change rapidly in the gift business, and so should your merchandise.

Take your time finding outstanding sidelines that are associated with or inspired by books (refer to Chapter 4) and be sure they're unusual — not the stuff you can find at the local drugstore or superstore. Some sidelines can be displayed on *spinner racks* (freestanding displays that sometimes come gratis in exchange for a minimum order; you can also purchase spinners, as shown in Figure 5-1, from suppliers like Clear Solutions). Always think about traffic flow and remember not to clutter up the store with racks. Another important display area is your *cash-wrap* or *point of sales* (POS) area.

Depending on the space you have at your cash-wrap (see Chapter 7 for more on this checkout area), you may want to display impulse items, single titles that are staff favorites, or music that's playing on the store sound system.

Figure 5-1: Spinner racks, spinnin' around. _____

Chapter 6

Taking Stock: Managing Your Inventory

In This Chapter
▶ Reviewing your computerized inventory-control system
▶ Knowing what, how much, and how often to reorder
▶ Creating a lean, mean delivery area and stockroom
▶ Knowing when — and whether — to send returns

*I*nventory management: You either love it or you hate it, but you know it's a reality of the bookselling business. How well you manage your inventory can make a tremendous difference in whether your bookshop is profitable.

✔ If you order too many copies of a book that doesn't sell, you use up valuable shelf space that may be put to better use with other titles.

✔ If you sell out of a book and don't reorder it right away, you lose several sales in the days while the hot, new title is still selling well. This can happen with backlist titles (refer to Chapter 5), too, if you're not ordering on a regular, timely basis and in response to sales.

✔ If a customer is looking for a particular book you have but can't find on the shelves, you lose a sale, and potentially, a customer. In the best-case scenario, you special-order the book for the customer and she waits patiently for it to arrive. Meanwhile, you've accumulated ordering and labor expenses while the original book is sitting mis-shelved and unsold.

✔ If you order quickly but the delivery sits in your stock-room for four days, you've just lost four days of sales for all of the books in that shipment. The publisher or whole-saler doesn't care that you're too busy to unload the ship-ment and generates an invoice for the books. The end result is that you have the books in house, you haven't sold any of them, and the invoice is already on its way.

Those scenarios — repeated often enough — can lead to seri-ous problems managing cash flow (see Chapter 13) and paying your bills and may even lead to the demise of your bookshop.

This chapter helps you find tips, tricks, and techniques for managing your inventory and stockroom, knowing when to reorder, and deciding whether to make returns.

Making Sure That Your System Works for You

Perhaps some tiny bookstore in Outer Mongolia still uses a paper system to manage inventory, but everyone else has switched to a computerized system.

If you're considering switching to a different system, keep in mind that a good computerized inventory system offers the following features:

✔ **Ease of use:** Above all, make sure that selling books to cus-tomers is easy. Your computer system should be invisible to your customer at the checkout and friendly to you and your staff in all operations. After you feel comfortable with the sales portion of the system, look into other areas. Is it easy to create an order for a publisher or wholesaler? Is receiving products a simple process? What reports does the system generate? Do you need the ones it generates, and can it generate the one(s) you need?

✔ **Flexibility:** Can you load other software on your inven-tory control computer(s) or does your system require dedicated equipment? Can you link your system to a reference database such as *Books in Print?* Can you use the modem only for ordering or can you also access the Internet?

✔ **Technical support:** Ideally, you want a system that doesn't require much support, but when you need technical help, you want someone who will walk you through problems.

✔ **Automatic backup:** Be prepared for disaster. When Waterstone's Booksellers in Boston, Massachusetts, suffered a major fire, backup tapes (kept in a fireproof safe) allowed employees to have the inventory system back up and replacing lost books in a matter of hours.

Reordering: What, How Much, and How Often?

After a book sells, you have to determine whether to order one more, ten more, or no more.

Every day, look at your inventory reports and walk around your store to see which categories are selling. Stay on top of your strongest categories — fiction, nonfiction, hardcovers, new paperbacks, mystery, children's, cooking, branded series, and so on — that consistently result in top sales. While an inventory system can communicate what sells and what doesn't, stocking a store isn't that simple: What your store physically looks like determines — at least in part — whether, what, and how much to reorder.

Make sure that you don't order merely *to space* (filling a space in your shop) but that you order *to sales* (looking at how well categories and specific titles have sold in the past). If you find that too much space is allocated to an underperforming section, consider shrinking the space and giving it to another section that is performing well or beyond expectations.

If you tend to overspend, establish a preset *open-to-buy* budget for every day, week, or month. For example, in the month of February, you have x dollars to spend on books. As you order during February, subtract the dollar amount from your budget. When you reach $0, stop ordering!

Knowing what mix of books and sidelines to order comes with experience. Chances are, if you're new to bookselling, you're a little overwhelmed by all of the possibilities. If you're an old hand at bookselling, however, you almost instinctively know what, how much, and when to order.

I say "almost instinctively" because even the saltiest old bookseller makes a mistake from time to time, and you can't let that fear immobilize you. If you're not sure what to order — or how much or how often — this section gives you some basic advice.

Knowing what to reorder

In order to know what to order, you need to do your homework. You've already placed your initial orders based on your review of publisher's catalogs and your best guess (refer to Chapter 5). As publication time draws nearer, you want to act as a sponge, soaking up as much additional knowledge and information as you can.

Industry magazines and Web sites give you an opportunity to scan the culture and hunt for additional titles that are likely to appeal to your core customers. *Publisher's Weekly* (PW) is the old standby for booksellers. Each week, PW provides an industry forecast, and its periodic articles on trends in book buying are extremely useful, as well.

Depending on your store's focus, you may want to read any or all of the following publications, in addition to PW:

- ✔ *New York Times*
- ✔ *New York Review of Books*
- ✔ *The New Yorker*
- ✔ *London Review of Books*
- ✔ *Times Literary Supplement*
- ✔ *Newsweek*
- ✔ *The Nation*
- ✔ *Atlantic Monthly*
- ✔ The largest regional paper in your geographic area

You can read these publications in print form or in some cases, on the Internet. *Publisher's Weekly,* for example, e-mails a daily version (www.publishersweekly.com), as does *The New York Review of Books* (www.nybooks.com). If you prefer getting your industry news online, consider non-print publications, such as Bookselling This Week (www.bookweb.org/news/btw), Book Sense (www.booksense.com), Publisher's Lunch (www.caderbooks.com), Salon.com (www.salon.com), and Holt Uncensored (www.holtuncensored.com).

If you're overwhelmed by all that reading plus your day job (you know — managing the store, lining up events, and so on), divide the publications among your employees so that they're all read religiously. Even if you employ just one or two book-sellers, you'll take some of the pressure off yourself while establishing respect for your employees' opinions and tastes.

Don't rely on industry magazines and Web sites to do frontlist buying. Reviews of books come out late in the game, after you should have already ordered important frontlist titles (see Chapter 5). If you order in response to reviews, you may end up waiting for the book while your customers purchase it else-where. Industry magazines can be extremely useful to your frontlist buying, however, in that they often look at book-buying trends and forecasts. As for magazine reviews, use them to make some last-minute decisions about frontlist titles just before they come out. For example, you may decide to place a second order to meet demand. You may also look for good reviews of books you missed in your initial order and place an order immediately.

Industry magazines and Web sites aren't a substitute for your instincts and experience with customers. If you have a gut feeling that a book won't work in your store, don't order it — even if it receives a rave review in PW!

In addition to reviewing industry publications, use the follow-ing resources to determine what new and backlist titles to add to your mix.

> ✔ **Browse online independent bookstores.** Check out stores like Tattered Cover Book Store in Denver, Colorado (www.tatteredcover.com) and Powell's Books at sev-eral locations in Oregon (www.powells.com).

Whenever you get a chance, physically visit other bookstores, too, to discover what's sizzling at other shops.

✔ **Browse reading-group information.** Choose from Random House, Simon & Schuster, Wiley Publishing, and other big-name publishers.

✔ **Think seasonally.** Plan not only for holidays (Christmas, Valentine's Day, Mother's and Father's day, and so on) but for seasonal events, as well:

- Winter's cabin fever may bring out customers browsing for novels, soup cookbooks, and weight-loss books.

- Spring may bring a need for landscaping and flower books and for customers planning their summer travel.

- Summer is a time for home remodeling, outdoor grilling, and a variety of outdoor sports.

✔ **Bank on local events and authors.** In the weeks or months leading up to a local road race, order books about running. During a local festival, stock books written by local authors and arrange for appearances several times a day.

✔ **Look for price points.** If the mass market book is $4.99, buy several. But if the mass market book is $7.99 and the trade edition is $12.99, opt for a few copies of the trade book, which is very close in price to the mass market book and is nearly always much nicer looking.

Keep in mind that, because you can't stock every English-language book published, you have to be selective about which books you do carry.

Knowing how much to order

To determine whether and how much to reorder, look at sales history and sales potential. If you're ordering weekly, you have to know what sold the previous week. With most computerized inventory-management systems, you can choose a particular time frame (for example, the weekend, the last two weeks, or year to date) or a category (such as new title hardcovers) and ask the computer to make a recommendation for reordering. Some booksellers shudder at the concept of letting the computer place the order, but remember that most systems are only using the following formula:

> Quantity *sold* in the time frame you determine
>
> – Quantity you have *on hand* or on *the way*
>
> = Quantity you need to reorder if the book continues to sell at its current rate

This type of formula is a time-saving way to jump-start your ordering. What you add to the mix is your own perspective and your bookselling expertise. When you reorder, incorporate the ideas of rent, inventory turns, and sales velocity.

Dear book: Your rent is due

Every book in your store needs to pay for itself. Think in terms of prime real estate — the front display area, for example, is where you want your primo books, the ones customers will recognize. This location isn't where you want your books that need a good push; instead, you want your noteworthy books or basics that always sell well, or books that your sales staff stands behind with personal recommendations. If a book isn't paying the rent, you may want to evict it — and you certainly don't want to reorder it.

Or, you may decide to keep the book anyway because its presence makes your store a better place for booklovers. For example, you may stock a literary classic that sells only one copy a year, but you feel you have to carry it. You simply can't be out of that book if a customer comes in looking for it. In cases like this, make sure that you have other books that pay a higher rent. Perhaps your bestseller section funds your poetry weakness, or your paperback fiction underwrites the art books you know will sell during gift-giving season.

You can't think of certain sections in the same rent-paying terms as others, but you do need to make certain that your overall inventory is paying for the space it occupies. In other words, you can choose to keep a title that sells only once a year, but be aware that you're making not only a literary decision, but also an economic choice that affects your bottom line.

For every book: Turn, turn, turn

An *inventory turn* refers to each time a book is sold. The dream of every independent bookseller is to see each book turn three times a year. In reality, however, your bestseller section may have an average turn of seven times in hardcover and fifteen in paperback, while poetry turns once per year. Still, look for your average turn to be between two and three times, weeding out any low-turning titles or categories when possible.

Operating at the speed of sales

Think in terms of *sales velocity*, which means looking at whether the title is gaining momentum, remaining static, or decreasing in sales. Ask yourself the following questions:

- ✔ Is the title at the top of its game, or is it waning?

- ✔ Could you have sold more copies if you'd had them on hand? Look for sales patterns over a given time that's something like, one sale one week, zero the next, one the next, zero the next, and so on. You're probably under-ordering, and during those zero periods, you could have sold copies.

- ✔ When did you run out (check the date sold and the sales pattern)?

- ✔ Has the book been hanging around forever, and you've just been praying for a buyer (check the invoice date)?

If the book has high sales velocity, be more aggressive with your orders. If the book has been around for a while, cross that reorder off your list.

Knowing how often to order

How often to order depends on what you're ordering and from whom: publishers or wholesalers (refer to Chapter 5 for more on deciding whether to reorder from wholesalers or publishers).

- ✔ **Order from publishers once a week.** Publishers traditionally give a better discount than distributors do and often ship for free (refer to Chapter 5 for the lowdown on ordering from publishers or wholesalers). In addition, when you have a great relationship with a rep and order directly from a publisher, you have someone to call on when your order isn't right. But the lead time for books shipped directly from the publisher is often long: five days to two weeks (or more). Therefore, many successful bookstores order from publishers about once a week.

Consider setting aside one day each week for the five publishers you order from most (Monday is Simon & Schuster, Tuesday is Wiley, and so on). Doing so can simplify your delivery system, because your orders from one publisher will tend to arrive all on one day.

✔ **Order from wholesalers daily or every other day.** Special orders (see Chapter 9) and books that are really hot are best purchased from wholesalers: The books come in, sell quickly, and lead to fast profits. Some stores order from wholesalers daily, replenishing what sold the day before, especially around the holidays. Depending on the size of your order, you may receive books ordered from a wholesaler the next day. If you're located in a more remote location, you may have to wait a little longer for your books, perhaps three days. In exchange for quick turnaround, however, you sacrifice discount points: Instead of the 43 to 46 percent you may receive from publishers, most wholesalers offer a standard 40- to 42-percent discount, with an additional point or two on a single title if you order five or more and meet the overall shipping minimums.

If time is in short supply, prioritize: Order special orders first, then strong-selling new titles (especially those with heavy publicity attached or with approaching laydown dates — see Chapter 8), then backlist books that sold the previous week.

Mondays are traditionally heavy ordering days: You place special orders that came in over the weekend and order based on what was depleted in hot weekend sales.

Most booksellers give new books a three- to six-month sales and promotion window, but that window is getting smaller all the time. So-called *instant books* (books driven by current events) may have only a one- or two-week window of top sales potential. If you order a flash-in-the-pan title from a publisher, which can take five to seven days, sales may have slowed down considerably (or be dead) by the time the order arrives. Order these types of titles from wholesalers.

Accepting Deliveries and Keeping Your Stockroom Efficient

Although receiving merchandise isn't a full-time job at most independent bookstores, you want someone (or, perhaps, more than one person) who's trained to log in orders (the date, who the shipment is from, how many cartons, reference PO, and so on). Some booksellers sticker every book as it comes in; others feel they save time by installing a wand that reads preprinted bar codes.

Unless your space constraints are overwhelming, avoid receiving books at the cash-wrap area. Instead, create a receiving area that has its own computer and workstation, preferably off the sales floor. You'll have less receiving errors, avoid cluttering the cash-wrap area, and minimize the risk of a newly delivered special order winding up in the hands of the wrong customer who happens to be asking about that particular title just as the shipment is being logged in.

Almost all publisher and wholesaler packaging includes your purchase order number on the mailing label. Use your purchase order (PO) numbers to cue you as to the contents of a given shipment. For example, use SO as a prefix for a special-order shipment or EV and the date as the PO number of a shipment that contains books for an event. This way, if you're looking for a particular shipment for an author event, you can find it quickly.

Give receiving priority to special-order, new-title, and wholesaler shipments. Those boxes have the largest percentage of titles your customers want now.

Be wary of backorders. You have no choice but to backorder on frontlist, because you need to wait until the books are published (see more on frontlist buying in Chapter 5). On backlist titles, your process is more efficient if you receive one shipment and one bill, so cancel any book that's not available (called *out-of-stock*) when you place your order, and then reorder it from another source. This approach is called *cascading out-of-stocks*. Many booksellers cascade publisher out-of-stocks to a wholesaler for their next order, and vice-versa.

Don't get behind! Publishers will soon be calling for money (so you have to pay), but you're not making money if books aren't out on the sales floor.

Making Happy Returns

Just as you need to focus on what's selling, you need to know what's not selling at all! You want to return these titles to make way for new ones.

Publishers sell you their books on the assumption that you'll then sell their books to your customers. But some books just don't sell, or they sell well below expectations — and publishers don't want you to get stuck with books that don't sell. The thinking goes that you'll get scared off of that publisher and not want to order more of their products. So, most publishers allow you to *return* merchandise and get credit for it after a certain number of days on the shelf (usually three months, but sometimes up to six months or more).

This means that you can make mistakes or have a bad season and still emerge relatively unscathed. However, your money is tied up in inventory (because you usually get a credit, not cash, for your returns), so you can't use that "money" to pay the light bill or order more sidelines.

You pay all shipping costs to return products, and because books weigh so much, this cost is expensive. Your labor costs have to be factored in, too. When the book first arrived, you unpacked, shelved, and tried to sell it. To return it, you generate a returns list, pull the book, repack it, and ship it. In some cases, you may be better off marking down the book (refer to Chapter 5). In other cases, you need to bite the bullet and get it out of your store and back to the publisher.

Keeping a book that never moves (that is, *not* returning it) is expensive, too. Your store has limited shelf space, and if a title that isn't selling is taking up an inch or two of shelf that a better performer could take over, you're better off returning the book(s).

Part III

Selling Books and Serving Your Customers

The 5th Wave   By Rich Tennant

"Your new book, 'Help-My Head's Caught in a Pipe' has been called by some to be semi-autobiographical. Can you comment on these rumors?"

In this part . . .

You find out more about the reason you went into bookselling in the first place: to sell books to booklovers. You get a grip on how to merchandise your products, get a buzz going about certain books, manage events, come up with low-cost marketing plans, get your hands on co-op money, get more deeply involved in your community, handsell books to your customers, and establish an exciting bookstore Web site. Whew! All that in this part alone.

Chapter 7

Setting the Mood: Your Store's Ambiance

*C*ustomers are looking for a place to spend their time (and, perhaps, their money), and you want to put your bookshop on their radar. For most of your customers, shopping for books isn't a chore, it's a pastime they enjoy. They don't come to your store only to buy books (although, by golly, you hope they leave with some!); they come for the experience. If you can make that experience one that customers look forward to and can't wait to repeat, they'll choose to spend both their time and their money at your shop. This chapter helps you make your store into a store that customers can't wait to experience.

You see yourself as competing with Internet bookstores, a couple of chain bookstores in your area, and the price club a few miles away, right? Well, yes and no. Those venues are the other places at which people tend to buy books, but don't think of your customers only in terms of where and how they spend money on *book* purchases. Think, also, of where else your customers spend their time and their money on *all* events.

Suppose, for example, that a couple wakes up on a Saturday morning and finds a blissful unplanned day ahead of them — no work, no home-improvement tasks, no family obligations; just time to relax, be entertained, and have fun. What might they do with their time and how might they spend their money? They might

- ✔ Go to the mall and spend all day shopping and, perhaps, having lunch at the food court.
- ✔ Head to the beach or the ski slopes and spend the entire day there.
- ✔ Go out for an early lunch, followed by a matinee at a movie theater.
- ✔ Pack a light bag and go hiking for several hours.
- ✔ Spend the day playing golf.
- ✔ See whether they can catch a ballet performance, live theater production, or an opera event.
- ✔ Attend (or watch on TV) a major league or college baseball, football, hockey, or basketball game.
- ✔ Spend several hours at an art or history museum.
- ✔ Head for the local coffee shop and sit down for a leisurely read of the day's newspaper.
- ✔ Drive around and look at fall colors.
- ✔ Go to the library and read this month's editions of all the magazines they carry.
- ✔ Stay in and spend the day watching cable and ordering pizza.

Except for the library, coffee shop, and, perhaps, the mall (if it has a bookstore) — and all of those are a bit of a stretch — none of the options facing this lazy-day-Saturday couple appears to be in direct competition with you. But the reality is that every single possible way to spend time *is* your competition. You're competing for a slice of these customers' time pie, and you need to get your store on their top-ten list of ways to spend a day, an afternoon, or an evening.

How do you do that? By making your store inviting — fun, comfortable, surprising in its offerings, and a venue for exciting events. Provide whatever you feel is necessary to make your shop a magnet for your customers. Alongside floor-to-ceiling books, provide comfortable chairs and couches, coffee tables and reading lamps, fun toys and play areas in the children's section, and areas that can be cleared out for large events. Make your shop a place where your customers want to spend time, and a place unique enough from their other choices that it stands out in their minds.

Think of your shop as the library — or, perhaps, even the home — that your customers have always wanted but couldn't afford. Your shop is an extension of their own homes and lives.

Establishing a Motif

Motif is just a fancy way to say "style," and every bookshop's motif is unique. Independent bookstores comes in all shapes and sizes and are housed in all sorts of locations, from an urban storefront in a centuries-old building to a suburban strip-mall location; from a log cabin in a resort area to a stunning Spanish Mediterranean-style building with an outdoor courtyard.

One bookshop design can't possibly fit every independent bookstore; instead, you need to assess the following:

- ✔ **What's the local flavor of your surrounding area?** If you're in an urban area, a log cabin probably isn't going to be your best bet. Think about the style of the surrounding buildings and the architectural heritage in your area to determine whether you can draw upon it.

- ✔ **What feeling do you want to create?** If you're trying to create a hip hangout, try bold colors, curving walls, and sleek, contemporary display units. If you want to offer a comfortable, living-room-like setting, provide overstuffed chairs, a fireplace or two, and soft, muted tones. If your bookshop is meant to be a cultural gathering place, be sure it's ready for large events and designed so that casual conversations can happen all over the store.

  Constantly remind your customers that yours is an independent bookshop. You aren't Borders, Barnes & Noble, Costco, or Sam's Club: Those stores provide a certain value to your customers, but it's different from the value that you offer. Make your store's ambiance stand out from that of the chains, just as your service and selection are unique from those superstores.

- ✔ **What's your personal taste?** Don't create a bookshop that doesn't suit you, or you won't want to spend time there. At the same time, remember that you're creating a retail space, not a residence. You want your store to appeal to you and to the many others who visit it, too. So, stretch your taste in creating your surroundings the same way you stretch your taste when selecting books to fill your shop.

✔ **What's the reality of your location and budget?** If you love big windows but are in a location that has tiny ones (or worse, none at all), make do: Light your store with natural but powerful bulbs that give the look of sunlight; create a beautiful display as you walk in that uses glass and bold colors.

Your store isn't Disneyland! Your motif must be organic to the building and individual space you're in, your customer base, your own taste, and your budget. If you're not sure how to pull those details all together, see whether you can hire an architect or bookstore consultant to help you jazz up your style. These professionals may be more affordable than you think and may be able to help you utilize more of your store space, such as the long, narrow areas that many strip-mall locations have to live with.

Don't overlook your floors as a source of comfort, beauty, and fun. Customers are most comfortable — that is, they stay longer and buy more books — when they have carpet underfoot. If you love the look of hardwood, consider combining wood and carpet, or look into alternative floor options with more cushioning. When you select your floor covering, think about sound as well as the look. Lots of wood and stone surfaces make the space more noisy, whereas fabric and cork tone down the sounds.

Don't be afraid to use color. Although you want to impress your customers with excellent service and outstanding selection, you also want to create a fond visual memory of your store. Color is also a cheap way to update your look, even if you're not ready to paint the walls or change the carpet. Consider bringing color into your category signs or asking a local artist to create a mural in the kid's section. If you're not confident selecting and matching colors, hire someone to help you.

Decorating doors and windows

Can you picture the ideal bookshop in your head? It doesn't have to be *your* shop — in fact, it probably isn't — but it has to be a store that welcomes you from the outside. What do you see?

✔ Big windows filled with charming book displays?

✔ A bright-red, eye-catching wooden door?

✔ A red-and-white striped awning over the doorway?

✔ An engraved wooden sign with your shop's name?

Beautiful, isn't it? Okay, now back to reality. Although some stores have been able to pull off this sort of dripping-with-charm entrance, most can't, either because of the limitations of their locations or because of budgetary constraints.

Rather than focusing on some ideal bookstore, think about what's practical for you and what will look inviting to your customers.

No matter how beautiful your store, ambiance alone isn't enough to sustain you — you also have to provide exceptional service on your well-targeted selection. By developing all three elements of your store to their fullest potential, you can successfully compete. If you're providing exceptional service and selection but don't currently have the most beautiful bookshop or most obvious sign, take heart. Big, interesting windows on a bookshop that exudes charm are a terrific way to draw customers, but if your store is simply clean, comfortable, and serves people's needs, word of mouth will spread.

Deciding How to Display Your Products

Just as hundreds of different bookshop designs exist, you can find hundreds of ways to display your products. However, all of these ways to display your products can be categorized roughly into two areas: products displayed on freestanding units (*displays*) and products organized by category.

An independent bookshop is all about self-discovery. The way that you display your books communicates to customers what books are important to you. The books you put on your front counter tell your customers that this store has a certain sensibility. Don't display all of the same books that the chain bookstore around the corner displays. Instead, make your selection unique, so that customers discover something. (Refer to Chapter 5 for more on selecting your frontlist titles.)

Your selection drives your displays. If you order enough of a title to face it out on a shelf or a little more to create a stack on a table, that's how you or your staff ultimately display them. So, in some sense, you're deciding when you order your frontlist titles how those books will be displayed months down the road.

Placing merchandise on shelves, by category

You're going to place the majority of your books on bookshelves, by category, because this is the most efficient use of the limited space in your bookshop. (No bookstore will ever have enough space for all the books you'd like to carry.) Bookshelves are also the easiest way for your customers and your staff to find books.

The categories you choose for your store are based on what you know your customers want to see when they visit you (refer to Chapter 4 for the lowdown on which categories to carry). You may have a large section on Buddhism or yoga, and not a single book on plumbing or perennials. And another store may have just the reverse. You get to decide.

Visual merchandising (or sometimes just *merchandising*) is a catch-all phrase used by retailers to describe the way you organize, display, and sell products. In big department stores, a team of people is often in charge of visual merchandising — you've probably seen them putting up the Christmas decorations right after Halloween. In most bookstores, everyone on staff does some visual merchandising — shelving books, for example. For your feature displays, you may find that one person has a better eye for display than do the others on your staff. Cut that person loose (with some guidelines), and you may be amazed at how he or she can transform your store!

Whatever your categories, however, keep the following in mind:

✔ **Your most popular categories need to be easily accessible, near the front door, or in their own wings of your bookshop.** If children's books are a hot category, don't stick them in the back of the store, out of the way. If cookbooks are what sell well for you, make your cooking sections the first ones you see when you enter the store. (Refer to Chapters 3 and 4 for information on how to nail down which categories are your most popular.) Conversely, if you sell only one book per year of each of the classics you stock, but have decided that classic literature is an important category for your store, you may want to give the section more prominence than the sales warrant, just to make a statement.

✔ **On the other hand, you can create destination categories.** *Destination categories* are popular categories that draw people to them, wherever they're located in the store. Some booksellers use this concept effectively — leading their customers through the store, up the stairs, and around the corner to find the much-visited remainder section or the great selection of fiction titles. Think of the big department stores and the way they route you through the cosmetics and perfume to get to the sportswear and bedding.

✔ **You don't have to shelve according to the publishers' categories.** If you're trying to shelve a book on coaching kids and the publisher's label says Sports, you're free to disregard that and shelve it under Parenting. A book on coin collecting that's labeled under Games may work better in Hobbies, or if you're really specialized, under Numismatics. Classics may go in the Children's and Adult sections.

✔ **Double-shelving is perfectly legal.** If a particular title fits in more than one of your categories, go ahead and shelve it in both. Just make sure that your inventory system keeps track of where all the title is so that you can easily find a copy for your customers.

Be sure that the person shelving is matching what's in the computer. If the computer thinks that you have two copies of a classic in children's and one in adult, but you really have three in adult, you may think, come inventory time, that you've lost (or *shrunk by*) two books. As much as possible, you want your shelves to match your computer, so develop a system whereby you can double-check under what categories your computer system thinks you're shelving each title.

✔ **Customers need to find other categories easily.** Sure, a customer can always ask you or any of your booksellers where your Numismatics section is located, but some people like to browse the store and wander from category to category. Make sure that your categories lead smoothly from one to the next — don't shelve Sports next to Judaica next to Home Decorating. Category groupings or *clusters* usually make the most sense — all the fiction categories grouped together, the parenting books near the kid's section, and so on.

Make sure that your categories are well signed. If possible, place signs so that they can be read from across the store. Ideally, you want customers looking in your windows to see category signage.

✔ **Don't be afraid to move categories — or get rid of them completely.** Don't move sections just for the sake of moving them, of course, but if a category is in prime real estate but doesn't sell much, *shrink* the category (provide fewer titles than you currently offer), or move it. Return what isn't selling and use the credit to start carrying something else. Refer to Chapter 6 for more.

✔ **Face out books that have attractive covers or that you know your customers will come looking for.**

✔ **Establish some sort of order to your shelving madness.** In most categories, books are shelved alphabetically by author. Sometimes, you may decide to shelve them alphabetically by subject, especially in sections like biography, travel, and sports. In these cases, shelve alphabetically by author within each subject category. In rare cases, you may want to shelve alphabetically by title — some booksellers prefer to shelve children's picture books this way, for example. Whatever way you choose to organize books in a section, just be sure that you and your staff follow the system, label the shelves, and create a system that makes sense to your customers.

Becoming a fixture in your community

Fixtures — bookshelves, tables, and other display units — are a necessity for successful booksellers. You can buy new, use antiques (or "classics" that will someday be antiques), or hire a local woodworker to make you custom shelving. If you do hire someone locally, however, be careful. While standard bookcases are designed to store books for personal use, bookstore fixtures are engineered to *display* books for sale. Fixtures made for the bookselling biz have special features, like a bottom shelf on bookcases that kicks out and up to show off products sitting *way* down there. Good bookstore fixtures are also designed to last over time, withstanding the heavy weight of books without bending or warping. Also, the ends of bookcases that are built for booksellers allow you to attach slat wall (see the "Displaying merchandise on tables and free-standing units" section), which allows you to produce unique displays on those bookcase ends. Clear Solutions (at www.clear solutionsdisplays.com) builds slat-wall accessories that maximize the display space you have there.

If you decide to upgrade your fixtures, go with the best you can afford. Lots of booksellers swear by Franklin Fixtures, a display fixture company that has been making bookstore fixtures for almost 30 years (www.franklinfixtures.com). Franklin's bookcases, tables, and other fixtures are made-to-order from standardized designs, which means that they cost less than custom work, but they can be easily modified to fit your space.

No matter where you obtain your displays, be sure that you have flexibility in moving some of your fixtures. Put tables or free-standing displays on casters, so that you can move them to make room for the crowds that come to your events.

Displaying merchandise on tables and free-standing units

Nearly every bookshop uses tables or other horizontal surfaces to display special books. These books may be merchandised in tall stacks or as one book surrounded by several other related books or by sidelines. These merchandising areas are called *feature displays*.

The following are some ways you may decide to feature titles on free-standing displays:

✔ **Keep track of what's in the media.** Has the latest book for a TV talk show or morning program just been announced? Make sure that it's on your front table or cash-wrap area (see the following section).

✔ **Establish a new-and-notable display.** Although the display can be an ongoing one, the items displayed can change weekly. Books in this display can be selected from your booksellers' favorites, the Book Sense bestseller list, awards (Edgars, National Book Awards, Newbery), and so on.

✔ **Tap into your local community's goings-on.** Is this the weekend of your town's annual festival? Put books about your city in a special display. Is this the annual pie-eating contest or chili cook-off? Put pie and/or chili cookbooks on display on the front table. Is a large road race going through your town? Display books about running.

✔ **Watch your calendar.** Is this Oscar week? Put books that led to Oscar award-winning movies on display. Is it March Madness? Display books about basketball on your front table. Is this Black History Month? Create a display of books on prominent African Americans.

Also take advantage of every major holiday, for example:

- Valentine's Day — books about chocolate or relationships

- All religious holidays — books explaining that particular faith

- Flower-planting and outdoor seasons — books about flowers, composting, deck-building, and so on

- Memorial Day and July 4th — historical books

- Summer vacation — travel books

- Labor Day — books about the history of unions or the sociology of workplaces

✔ **Display by events:** Make tables of an author's books or books that complement those of an author who is making a store visit. After the visit is over, keep signed copies (for sale, of course) on display for a few days or weeks.

✔ **Display sidelines (refer to Chapter 4) with relevant books.** So, when winter's chill makes even the warmest-blooded customer think of hot beverages, prepare a small display of books about tea, coffee, and cocoa, along with coffee mugs, tea sets, and other related items. You may also want to set up a display that combines books with gifts and prices them as a set. For example, a hardcover book about salads that retails for $35 may be combined with salad tongs that sell for $40. By pricing them together at $75 in a Mother's Day display, you may be able to pick up an extra $40 in sales for no more work than selling only the book.

This idea is especially effective in your children's area. Grandparents often want to buy books as gifts, but they also don't want their grandchildren to yawn when they open them. By combining one or more books with a plush animal, game, puzzle, or CD, the gift may be more enticing to the youngster.

Many bookshops set up one front table that customers can't help but bump into as they walk in the store. The books on your front table can change daily, based on whatever's hot in the national media or in your small town.

Booksellers and other retailers often use vertical space to create feature displays. If you have an empty wall area in your store, consider installing slat wall. *Slat wall* is wood or laminate material with horizontal grooves, or slats. After slat wall is secured to the wall (and be sure it's well-secured — it is often heavy!), you can slip various display devices into the grooves. These devices are called *slat-wall inserts*. Usually made of clear Lucite, the inserts come in all sizes and shapes (see Figure 7-1). You can use an easel-shaped insert to create a display of single copies in an interesting geometric arrangement, or use a pocket-shaped insert to create a row of books or greeting cards. Some slat-wall inserts are small shelves — perfect for merchandising lightweight sidelines.

If you don't have any more wall space available, have a look at the ends of each aisle of bookshelves. You can also install a slat-wall end panel at the end of an *island* (a bookcase that isn't attached to a wall) and gain feature display space there, too.

You can create feature displays anywhere — on tables, on slat walls, in shop windows. You can also use *free display packs* (floor displays or displays that sit on shelves or tables to highlight features titles).

Figure 7-1: Slat-wall with inserts.

Merchandising Your Cash-Wrap Area

The area affectionately known as *cash-wrap* is where your customers pay for their purchases before leaving the store. The basic setup for a cash-wrap area includes the following:

- 🖛 A cash register, usually computerized
- 🖛 A workstation for taking special orders, checking inventory, and consulting your reference database
- 🖛 Bags in which to wrap customers' purchases
- 🖛 Any giveaways, such as bookmarks imprinted with your store's name
- 🖛 Business cards or brochures

Those items are the basics, but if you included only those items in your cash-wrap area, you'd be taking a strict minimalist approach. The reality is that cash-wrap areas usually also include the following:

✔ More cash registers.

✔ Gift wrap, tape, and tags for free gift wrapping service (see Chapter 9).

✔ Signs or posters for events, Book Sense Bestsellers, and/or Book Sense gift certificates (see Chapter 8) affixed to cabinet bases or to the wall behind the cash-wrap area.

✔ Products, particularly impulse items, such as the following:

- Copies of a hot-selling book

- One or two staff recommendations

- Magazines or newspapers

- Pens

- Note cards, greeting cards, and/or stationery

- Blank journals

- Coffee mugs

- Candy

- Refrigerator magnets

- High-quality bookmarks

- Magnifiers and glasses

If you merchandise the cash-wrap carefully, you can make the check-out a prime display area that leads to sales. Avoid the tendency to put too much stuff in the vicinity of the cash register. Keep it stocked with special items, change those items frequently, and make sure that the display space and the check-out space are always clean and well-organized.

Because customers who need a particular book often make a bee-line from the front entrance to the cash-wrap area, place your cash-wrap close to your front entrance(s) and make it easily recognizable to a new customer. If you're sitting in the cash-wrap area when a customer walks in, get up, greet the customer warmly, and ask whether you can be of assistance.

Chapter 8

Getting Customers in the Door

*G*etting people in the door is critical to your success. If you have a tremendous selection, beautiful window displays, lively play area for kids, comfortable chairs, and generous refreshments, but you can't get customers to walk through the doorway, you won't stay in business long.

This chapter tells you how to get people excited about your store, how to stage events, and how to partner with Book Sense to attract even more customers. It's full of great ideas from booksellers across the country, ideas you can put to use in your store right away.

Generating a Buzz

The best way to get customers in the door is to give them a compelling reason to come in. So, what's your compelling reason? Do you have a hot title that you want everyone to get excited about? Do you serve the best coffee in town? Have you scheduled an intriguing event? Figure out your compelling reasons, and then generate a buzz about it.

You can generate a buzz about your store — or about a particular book or event — without spending a lot of money. This section shows you how.

To trickle a national buzz down to your community bookstore, keep up with the titles in the media spotlight. Keep tabs on books reviewed on National Public Radio (NPR), in newspapers, and in magazine articles. Find out what books the morning talk shows are pushing and what authors Oprah has scheduled. The media listings in *Publisher's Weekly* can be a helpful resource, and Ingram's I-Page also offers a media section.

Advertising within your store

When you "advertise" within your store, you aren't necessarily drawing new customers to your door, but you are promoting your store as a place that customers want to be. You can create a buzz within your store — about new books, an upcoming event, or a favorite title. To draw attention to particular products or events in your store, try out some of the following ideas:

✔ Create a permanent display area that showcases upcoming events. Include a calendar, a photo of each author or speaker, and books or book jackets.

✔ Place books that tie-in with events on displays throughout the store, along with information about the events.

✔ Create signs, flyers, posters, or banners about events or new releases. The sky's the limit, but be careful not to clutter your store (which means that you have to be choosy) and make sure every sign has impact. Use heavy-weight paper with a scanner and a color printer to generate these impressive-looking (but inexpensive) in-store ads. Display the ads in a Lucite sign-holder or glue them to foam board that you can get at an art supply or crafts store. If you're not ready to invest in equipment to make your own, head down to your local printing or copy shop to see whether it can print 2' x 3', 3' x 4', or 5' x 8' signs. And remember, you may be able to get co-op money (see Chapter 5) to offset the costs of title or publisher-specific signs. (You may be able to hang flyers in the surrounding community, too, not just in your store.)

You may want to hang signs and banners for the hottest-selling new releases and nationally recognized authors who may come to your store, but don't stop there. Also advertise midlist authors and local writers with signs and banners. They'll appreciate your paying attention to them, and you'll generate larger crowds at these events.

✔ Hang shelf tags, sometimes called *shelf talkers,* for special books to which you want to draw customers' attention. Advertise these books on your Web site (see Chapter 10), and then put "As seen on the Web site" tags around your shop.

✔ Design a window display that promotes a certain book, author, or event. If you have the time and creative juices (or employ someone who does), consider changing your window displays every few days so that your window itself creates a buzz. If your window is exciting and fresh, people will come by just to see what's there.

Don't let your booksellers be the last to know about the great books and events that you're using to draw customers. Your booksellers have to be able to talk about and get excited about the book or event. From the time you know that an author's coming or a title is expected, keep booksellers up to date by giving them specific information about the book or the author and by making reading copies available to the staff. Also, talk to your staff about what's in the news — a big new release or a book-club selection on one of the network talk shows — and encourage them to share what they've seen or heard with you, too.

Sending announcements and newsletters

One of the most effective — and cheapest — ways to generate a buzz about a product or an event is to send e-mail reminders and newsletters to your customers. (If you link this information to your Web site, as discussed in Chapter 10, you don't have to put much content into the messages themselves, but can, instead, refer readers to your site.) Some stores send out weekly event e-mails and monthly electronic newsletters; others send an e-mail message a few days before each event and the day before the release of a new title. Check out Chapter 10 for ideas on getting customers to sign up for your e-mail announcements.

Buy ten, get one free!

Want to get customers back in your store again and again? Besides offering extraordinary customer service (which means, among other things, that you have the books readers want or can get them very quickly), consider giving customers a frequent-buyer card: For every ten books they purchase, they get a $10 or $15 gift certificate or a free book. With many computer cash-register systems, customers don't even have to keep a punch card in their wallets; instead, the computer adds up the right dollar amount spent or the number of books purchased and spits out the gift certificate or other information.

Also, give gift certificates whenever you're asked to contribute to any not-for-profit event. Instead of donating a book or sideline product, which doesn't give the recipient a choice, donate a gift certificate of $20 or $25. That way, you get a new customer into the store, looking at your selection.

Although you can send e-mails to your entire mailing list (and some smaller stores have lists in excess of 4,000 customers), you can also generate specific mailings about an author's new book or appearance to customers who, for example, purchased that author's books in the last year. That type of targeted marketing (more on this in Chapter 3) can have a tremendous impact on sales of new releases and on event attendance.

If a portion of your audience isn't comfortable online or simply doesn't check e-mail often enough to make the messages timely, send weekly, semi-monthly, or monthly postcards announcing events or new releases. These mailings don't have to be professionally printed — a laser printer and a simple postcard design is enough to attract attention. If you find that you send enough of these postcards and need them to stand out, check with your local printer to find out how much printing a copy of the book jacket on one side of the postcard will cost. Another option is to purchase a color laser printer, which can be extremely cost-effective after the initial investment.

Taking advantage of free publicity

In order to generate free publicity, you have to think like the media: What books, events, book-industry information, business briefs about your store (new hires, promotions, expansion, remodeling) will their readers, listeners, and viewers want to hear about? You have to create news and make it compelling, keeping in mind the local media's customer base and political stance.

To obtain free publicity regularly, you have to make a commitment to a newspaper or radio station (and, if appropriate in your area, a TV station). Doing so means developing a close working relationship with one reporter or editor, giving him or her as much information as possible, and finding a hook that makes your story compelling to readers. You need to develop a fantastic relationship with the local media to fully leverage this free source of attention.

Making a commitment also means paying for advertising in the local media from time to time. The media you support with paid advertising will support you with all the free publicity they can give you. If you never advertise in the local newspaper or on local radio, you can't expect much in the way of freebies.

Don't always go to the same contacts at your media outlets; rather, target your stories to the editor or outlet that will be most interested. For example, if an AM station is heavily into sports, they are the perfect partner for a baseball book or an event for an athlete/author. If a newspaper or TV station focuses its coverage on schools, use it for school book fairs and for parenting events.

Send press releases about every single event and send public service announcements (PSAs) about every not-for-profit venture in which you're involved. Create a simple form with your letterhead and list who, what, where, and when about the event, service, or products. Not only do you want to make the event compelling, but you also want to use as few words as possible and make the release or PSA short and to the point.

If you're having trouble getting free publicity, consider teaming up with other organizations (universities, public schools, not-for-profits) that may have a greater pull with the media.

Utilizing paid advertising

Yes, you can pay for advertising, too! Advertise in your local daily paper, in artsy or cultural papers, in university or high-school papers, on your local public radio stations, and on other radio and TV stations that are affordable.

Keep in mind that you may be able to pay for your advertisement with co-op money — how much depends on the available funds, the size or length (in radio) of the ad, and your purchase commitment with a given publisher. (Refer to Chapter 5 for more on co-op dollars.) In addition, by teaming up with other booksellers or retailers in your area, you may be able to pay for a large ad that advertises a particular event or group of related products (featuring a home-building book, alongside the products of your local lumberyard, for example).

Consider going to a professional advertising company and asking it to come up with a consistent advertisement into which you can drop relevant information. For around 2,000 well-spent dollars, you can receive a design for your ads at all the popular ad sizes, plus letterhead, bookmarks, business cards, gift certificates, and bags. This way, customers immediately recognize that your ad comes from you, and you save time designing each ad.

Staging Events

Staging events (see Figure 8-1) is both exhilarating and frightening. After all, what if you stage an event and no one comes? Or, what if half the town comes, and you don't have room for everyone? Before scheduling any event, ask yourself the following key questions:

- ✔ Is this an event you can handle in terms of the projected size of the audience and the advertising required?
- ✔ Do you have books (tie-ins) you can sell at the event?
- ✔ Will the event be compelling to your customers?
- ✔ Is this event something the local media would want to write about?

If you answer "yes" to all four questions, you have a great event in mind. If not, consider partnering up with an organization that has a larger space and/or a staff that can help with planning. Also, consider changing the event to one your customers will come out for and buy books about. The following sections can help you consider the types of events you can arrange.

Figure 8-1: The Dummies Man pays a visit to Davis-Kidd Booksellers in Nashville, Tennessee.

Many booksellers serve refreshments (appetizers, beverages, snacks) during events, and customers have come to expect them. You want your event not to simply be a distraction in your store but to be a *destination* for your customers, who plan to come and who look forward to the time spent at the event.

Author appearances

Author appearances are far and away the most popular bookstore event, but they vary considerably in what the author actually *does* when he or she is in the store, such as:

- Reading a passage from a recent book.
- Talking about why he or she wrote the book and what the experience was like.
- Signing books — some bookshops never do signing alone, while others offer nothing but book signings.
- Engaging the audience with a Q&A session.
- Mingling with the audience.
- Giving a workshop on a recent book's topic.

Consider grouping similar authors or poets together in one event. The authors may feel more comfortable (less in the spotlight), and you'll likely get a larger crowd. You can ask each author to read from or talk about his or her work for ten

Promoting local authors

Many — although not all — bookshops give preference to local writers and see doing so as a part of their mission as community bookstores. Although a prominent national author is likely to draw a large crowd, so, too, can a regional author with a large gathering of family, friends, and colleagues.

If you have a lot of local authors or books about your geographic area, consider starting a rotating window display of just these titles. Local authors will know that your store is where they need to hold their events.

With local authors, don't worry too much about sales, but do think about traffic — you don't want to embarrass either an author or your store. Chances are, you can't possibly fit every local author into your schedule (or you wouldn't have time for national authors), so once or twice a month,

sponsor a local author's day that may include three or four events, and treat these authors especially well on their special day. Create a postcard or special e-mail describing the event and send it to the author-generated list of family, friends, and others. Hang a banner welcoming the authors.

Don't just support local authors in your events, but also in your inventory. You don't have to carry large quantities, but keep your store stocked with the books of local authors. Even consider carrying some titles that aren't traditionally published, such as poetry *chapbooks* (thin books or pamphlets) and fundraising cookbooks. Acquaintances of local authors want to know where they can get their books — the first words out an author's mouth when asked about that should be the name of your store.

minutes and schedule frequent breaks throughout the event so that customers can speak with their favorite writers one-on-one.

Make sure that both the audience and the authors have a good time. Don't worry about how many books sell, just take care of the authors and your customers.

Kids' events

Kids' events aren't just great fun, they're also good ways to build your business, because parents and grandparents buy a lot of books for children. You can be especially creative with events for children. Here are some ideas:

✔ **Story time:** Whether daily or twice a year, reading to kids always draws a crowd, although sometimes the crowds are so big that the event nearly shuts down the store. If you really want to torture kids but sell a lot of books, read the first chapter or two of an easy chapter book, and leave the rest up to them or their parents.

✔ **Harry Potter pajama parties:** Waiting until 10:00 the next morning to get your own copy of the latest Harry Potter book just doesn't work for most kids. They want that copy at 12:01 a.m. on the *laydown date,* the first date per publisher/bookseller agreements that the book can be distributed to customers (the book can be pre-sold but not given to customers). Have kids dress in their PJs and bring sleeping bags and pillows to the store while they wait for release of the book. They can hear from key chapters of the preceding book. After the mad late-night rush, stage a reading of the first chapter — if you can get the kids to sit still long enough, now that they have their own copies!

✔ **Themed breakfasts:** Several stores also open early on the Harry Potter laydown date and offer breakfasts, readings, and other events early in the morning. Also consider other breakfast events, such as American Girl events that offer readings or workshops on the historical period of the latest series.

✔ **Crafts events, after-school programs, and Saturday programs:** Any events you can plan that creatively occupy kids' time and make your store a destination for kids brings customers to your store and, eventually, reaps sales. During these events, you may read stories, offer snacks, and teach kids a craft to take home. You can also increase your events during school breaks, when kids may be bored. Try to make your store a place where kids want to come.

✔ **Author events:** Smaller marketing budgets mean that children's authors and illustrators can be difficult to secure for an event. If you do manage to snag an author, you can almost guarantee that he or she will be fun and exciting. Kids and their parents will line up for blocks for a favorite children's author or illustrator.

✔ **Kids book clubs:** See more about book clubs in the following section.

✔ **Cultural events:** Offer previews of performances around the city, including ballet, opera, other musical groups, theater, and so on. Give away a free pass to these performances as a door prize. These previews appeal to kids because they are engaging but short, unlike the two-hour-long evening version that parents may attend.

✔ **Writing contests:** Offer short-story and poetry contests centered around a word, phrase, theme, or other distinguishing feature. Offer prize money and try to get the schools involved so that classroom time is devoted to the contest. The results will range from the very serious to the downright hysterical.

If you have spare room in your store, invite parents to listen to a teacher or other professional discussing books for different ages and stages while their kids are occupied. Hand out bookmarks or other promotional materials that list great books for each particular age group.

Book clubs and reading groups

In many areas of the country, book clubs (also called *reading groups*) are hot right now, and many stores promote the clubs in the store and on their Web sites.

You or your staff members can help clubs get started in the following ways:

✔ If you have the space, let clubs meet in your store.

✔ Offer a discount to book club members who are buying the latest club selection.

✔ Offer to meet with book clubs to talk about suggested readings for the year or season.

✔ Go to the book club meeting the first time, lead it, and practice honest and respectful discussion.

✔ Lend audio tapes of author events to book clubs.

✔ List book club selections and meeting dates and times on your Web site.

✔ Tag selections in the store as book club titles.

✔ If you have a children's section, start a mother/daughter, father/son, or parent/child book club that merges your adult and younger customers. For many of these clubs, the kids are ages 11 to 15, and the books reflect that age group. Parents get a wonderful opportunity to better understand their kids' interests, values, and pressures.

✔ Organize book clubs that cover particular areas of interest to you or your staff but may not currently be in existence (for example, spiritual, peace and justice, poetry, or feminist book clubs).

✔ Start a new-title book club that reads and discusses your hottest frontlist titles or top selections from the Book Sense 76 (see the "Tapping into Book Sense" section later in this chapter for a discussion of this program).

Authorless events

Authorless events are practically limitless, but make sure to tie them in with books that you can sell.

Consider the following examples of authorless events, which are just the tip of the iceberg, if you're the creative type:

✔ Schedule health and well-being days, in which physicians, therapists, and other health-care professionals give workshops, do demonstrations, give massages, and so on.

✔ Offer a winter cabin-fever series, where local people who have done something unique give a short workshop on topics ranging from business ethics to Native American relationships to the earth to a Mount Everest fated climb.

✔ Plan a travel series that partners with a local travel agency and discusses a new destination each week or month; refreshments include airline food, such as peanuts, small pretzels, and soda.

✔ Pop plenty of popcorn once a week in March or April and offer events that have to do with gardening, sailing, or other outdoor event to get customers thinking about spring.

✔ Arrange a New Age fair with an astrologer, tarot card reader, palm reader, and other fun demonstrations.

✔ Present music in the store on certain nights, featuring local musicians. You may want to give the musicians gift certificates for playing and/or offer CD signings that promote each musician's work; some bookshops are seeing popular artists return for musical events because they're grateful for getting their start years before at the bookstore.

✔ Schedule opera wraps with a local opera company in the off-season. Have them discuss the upcoming season and explain the plots of the operas.

✔ Put on holiday events; for example, a St. Patrick's Day event that features Irish music, dancing, author signings, foods, and so on.

✔ Display art or photos that feature works from a local gallery that has recently changed exhibits but would like one more chance for potential customers to view the artwork.

✔ Team up with the monthly magazine in your urban area (many cities feature these glossy, well-edited publications) and do monthly events with the editors on the feature of the month. Joseph-Beth Booksellers partners with *Cincinnati Magazine* to put on monthly events in which customers meet with editors (and sometimes even the people featured in the articles) and discuss the issue. In addition, the bookstore puts on a wedding event that ties in with an annual bridal issue of the magazine.

✔ Partner with a public television or radio station and tie books to shows, such as *Masterpiece Theater, Fresh Air, Science Friday,* and so on.

✔ Offer food events, including wine-tasting (keeping in mind that you may have to obtain a special permit), cheese sampling, tasting of ethnic foods, and so on.

Off-site events

Off-site events may be too large to hold at your store, and groups who co-sponsor events may want to hold the events at their locations. However, one of the most common off-site events for independent booksellers is to sell books at conferences offered locally or in nearby towns. Conferences aren't easy, because you need to negotiate what percentage of your sales will go to the conference, send one or two employees (or yourself) to the conference with a good selection of applicable books, set up a cash register, and so on. You discover more about these unique sales opportunities in Chapter 9.

Besides conferences, writers' workshops are popular off-site events, often held at a university or camp. Writers' workshops, which range from one-day to more than a week, also take a tremendous amount of time and effort, but they are rarely disappointing. To run a successful writers' workshop (for kids or adults), bring in one or two national authors and more regional authors who are willing to work with burgeoning writers or give short lectures. (Partnering with a college or university, library, or summer camp takes some of the burden off of you.) You can also sell books about writing and books by the guest authors. Don't be surprised if you get attendees who just want to meet and listen to the writers, and have no desire to work on their own writing!

Another popular off-site event is any local festival. For these events, you generally set up a tent, booth, or table and sell books that relate to the topic (not a whole lot, but doing so gets the word out that you're at the event). You may even do some fundraising for a local charitable organization. If the event happens within the vicinity of your store, be sure to also staff your store that day and decorate the store in a way that's relevant to the local event. As a community bookstore, if you can spare the manpower, you want to fully participate in any event that's popular with your customers, from the local Polish festival to Earth Day to Cinco de Mayo celebrations. If you want to spruce up the event, see whether you can bring a national author to the festival or whether a regional author can put on a workshop that relates to the festival or time of year.

Communing with Your Community

You're part of a number of communities: a geographic community, a community of independent retailers, and perhaps a political or activist community, depending on the focus of your bookshop.

This section helps you link your role in those communities to increased traffic in your store and, perhaps, to increased sales. Although many booksellers are altruistic and simply want to help others in their communities, you can help others *and* make your business more visible in the process.

Establishing your store as a community meeting place

One of the best ways to get customers in the door is to open your doors to every group that wants to use your facilities, free of charge. If your bookstore is small, try to expand your space by placing tables outside for community members to use. Encourage only small groups to use your store, such as small book clubs and one-on-one literacy or school tutors.

If your space is larger, consider hosting receptions, encouraging not-for-profits to hold meetings, sponsoring church events, allowing home-based-business owners to hold small business meetings, and supporting book fairs (see Chapter 9) in which schools may get up to 15 percent of your sales to students and parents.

Many bookstore owners find that adding a coffeehouse expands the community space, making the store more of a place to hang out than to shop. Even if you don't have a café or coffee shop, however, you can still evoke the community feel simply by allowing as many groups as can fit to make your store their community center.

Regardless of how you set up your store, think in terms of traffic, not sales. You want to draw people in and sure, sometimes, they'll sit at your tables, use your bathroom, and even drink your free coffee or lemonade, but they won't buy a thing. Don't grind your teeth, because that's perfectly okay. Before long, that person's use of your store will turn into profits for you.

Developing sponsorships and not-for-profit partnerships

Without going bankrupt, try to donate to every cause that comes through your door, such as the following:

- ✔ Partner with a school, donating books to their libraries or summer reading programs.
- ✔ Make book donations to senior citizen centers, retirement communities, and hospitals.

✔ Sponsor a Little League team. You're contributing to the community — and the team is wearing your store's name.

✔ Sponsor annual fundraisers of not-for-profits, in which the group brings in authors, you sell books, and you donate a portion of the book sales back to the not-for-profit group.

✔ Give donations for raffles and fundraisers, for example, taking a coffee mug for your store and stuffing it with a generous gift certificate.

✔ Sponsor a local 10K race, Gus Macker tournament, or other athletic fundraiser and prominently display books on running, basketball, or whatever other sport you sponsor. (Also see whether your store's name can appear on the T-shirts.)

✔ Set aside space for a community bulletin board that displays housing notices, business advertisements, workshops and classes, and employment notices.

✔ Use the back of your bookmarks for community service — tips for healthy living, parenting ideas, phone numbers of crisis centers or other groups, directions to library events, and so on.

✔ Offer discounts for teachers and other public servants.

Joining business groups

If your business community includes a Chamber of Commerce or downtown business association, consider not only being a part of it, but also leading it. Being a prominent member of business groups makes your store visible and sets up partnerships with others in the community. For example, you may be able to establish a businessperson's breakfast at your store or other location that features a relevant author. Ticket prices include the price of a signed book.

Your political connections may also get you access to name authors for events at your store. You may even discover local authors and their books through your business connections.

You can also form relationships with people interested in good causes that are in sync with yours. You may actually be able to do more good works by acting in conjunction with other organizations than by working alone — you can leverage your involvement because you're banding together with other businesses or local nonprofits.

You may also be able to improve the area around your store through your involvement with business groups. Do you have problems with crime, parking, and so on? Use this network of business professionals to solve business problems. Everyone in your community is interconnected, so you need to work with others in your community.

Developing partnerships with other retailers

Booksellers have a lot in common with other small retailers, so consider partnering with the businesses in your area. If your local movie theater is independent, partner with the theater to sell books that relate to a particular movie and split the cost of advertising it. Builder's Booksource in San Francisco, California, specializes in books for and about building and remodeling houses, so that store has partnered with a local hardware store to send out bookstore information with hardware store bills.

Be mindful of whether you're supporting local businesses in your everyday decisions. Buy whatever you can locally, from your printing to your accountant to your payroll service. If you run a coffee shop, see whether you can buy from a local coffee roaster.

Tapping into Book Sense

Book Sense is a national network of independent booksellers who combine their strength and enhance their marketing clout through participation in an ongoing program created by ABA. Some components of Book Sense include

 ✔ **Book Sense 76,** bi-monthly listings of notable (sometimes quirky, but always delightful) books that are based on rec-ommendations from booksellers from around the country. The titles are presented in a professionally designed flyer that booksellers display in their stores to help customers find out about great books. Stores with Book Sense display their favorites from the Book Sense 76 alongside copies of the flyer: This type of cross-promotion helps customers discover new books. Because one independent book-seller's quote accompanies information about each title, customers also delight in searching for their local book-sellers' names and preferences in the Book Sense 76 list-ings. Customers know that titles in the 76 are good reading and have come to depend on that list and in-store displays for recommendations.

✔ **National advertising campaign** in prominent consumer publications. These ads often feature a book cover shot alongside a recommendation for that book by an inde-pendent bookseller (who is quoted in the ad). The adver-tisement directs readers to their local independent bookstores to purchase the title. Each ad features the Book Sense logo, which participating stores also display on their signs, on bookmarks, and in local ads. To see examples of recent ads, check out ABA's Web site at www.bookweb.org, click on General Information on the Book Sense logo, and then click on Book Sense Ads in Print. Although the titles are always selected by book-sellers, Book Sense ads are often partially subsidized by the publishers of the recommended title.

Stores that participate in the Book Sense program get a White Box every month that's jam-packed with cool stuff: advance reading copies from publishers, marketing mate-rials from Book Sense, and publisher's promotional infor-mation. Participating booksellers can also request galleys from publishers through a program called Advance Access. Some smaller bookstores that weren't on the map with major publishers have seen more visits from publishers' sales reps (refer to Chapter 5) since the pro-gram began — this is a result of independent booksellers being represented as a collective group, not as simply a single bookshop.

✔ **The weekly Book Sense Bestseller Lists,** which rank titles based on sales reported by a diverse range of independent bookstores across the United States. The list covers sev-eral categories and reflects the previous week of bookstore sales. Book Sense stores can release these lists to their local papers, so that customers can see what's selling at independent bookstores. Many bookstores set up Book Sense Bestseller displays in their stores and/or feature a selection of Book Sense Bestsellers on their Web sites.

✔ **A national gift certificate program,** which allows the customers of an independent bookstore in Georgia to buy bookstore gift certificates for relatives in Colorado to spend at their local bookseller. Booksellers report that the numbers of customers requesting Book Sense gift certificates rises every year.

✔ **Promotions and partnerships** — described in full-color posters — that are offered each year and focus on a particular book or author. For example, Book Sense teamed up with the History Channel and sponsored a *Fire on the Mountain* contest that featured the book and the subsequent docu-movie and asked bookstores from around the country to raise money for local firefighters. Andrea Avantaggio and Peter Schertz, owners of Maria's Bookshop in Durango, Colorado, participated in the Book Sense contest and won! They teamed up the local paper and the Durango Public Library and held three events in conjunction with the contest: a firefighter slide show (which sold out), an appearance by author John Maclean, and a preview of the docu-movie at the local theater before it was released to the public. In all, Durango firefighters received $2,500 as a result.

✔ **BookSense.com**, an optional Web site program available to Book Sense stores that lets you establish your own full-featured Web site with a minimum investment of time and money. See Chapter 10 for details.

The Book Sense program is free, although your store must qualify to be a member in the following ways:

✔ You must be a member of ABA.

✔ You must own a bookstore that has a bricks-and-mortar storefront location that's accessible to the public.

✔ A substantial portion of your sales must come from new trade books.

✔ You commit to promoting the Book Sense brand by including the Book Sense logo in your marketing materials and displaying the Book Sense logo on your front door.

✔ You agree to use Book Sense bags and display posters and brochures.

✔ You agree to sell and accept Book Sense gift certificates.

✔ You're expected to recommend titles for Book Sense 76 and report your sales for the Book Sense Bestseller List.

✔ You may choose to participate in BookSense.com.

Chapter 9

Understanding the Gentle Art of Selling

*S*elling books just doesn't feel the same as selling cars or appliances, does it? Unlike some salespeople, your job isn't to convince customers that their lives would be better if they bought a particular product or pressure them to buy a product from you at a certain price. That just isn't why you got into the bookselling biz.

Still, you have to sell products in order to make a living as a bookseller. In fact, in order for your store to thrive, you must be an expert at sales. But how do you do excel at sales without putting on a plaid jacket and getting all schmaltzy about "making you an offer to get your best deal at rock-bottom prices — this weekend only"?

You sell gently. You sell respectfully. And you sell for the long haul. That's why you won't find any hard-sell tactics in this chapter. Instead, you find out how to meet your customers needs and keep them coming back for more, all without ever uttering slogans like, "Have I got a deal for you!"

A Friend in Need . . .

Ultimately, you want to sell books. You just can't run a book-shop for long if you don't have money coming in and books going out. But if you're like many booksellers, you *hate* the idea of "selling" books. You'd rather create an atmosphere that customers will want to visit, hoping they'll buy simply because they like what they see. But this hands-off approach fails to recognize that customers have needs — and that they don't advertise their needs by carrying in a sign that says, "I'm look-ing for a book that will divert my attention from my stressful job" or "I want to find out more about my son-in-law's religion." If you don't find out what your customers need, you miss the opportunities to meet their needs with books and other prod-ucts. So, instead of thinking about "selling" to your customers, think about meeting your customers' needs.

Customers may come to your store for plenty of reasons other than purchasing a book (refer to Chapter 3 for more on the basics of meeting needs). They may come in to

- Socialize and interact with others
- Gather information
- Be entertained
- Seek a solution to a problem
- Rest or relax
- Divert their attention
- Fill someone else's need (as is the case with gift-buying)
- Find support
- Learn

Can you fill those needs? Sure you can. But first you have to know that they exist. You do that by engaging your customers in dialogue.

Suppose a customer walks in to your store and begins brows-ing. You sit in the cash-wrap area, acknowledge the cus-tomer's presence with a smile or a wave or even a gentle, "How are you today?" and allow her to browse. You feel good about the respect and latitude you're showing this customer by "leaving her alone" and figure she'll come to you if she has any questions.

Does this person have a need you can meet? You betcha, but you'll never know what it is, because you haven't engaged her enough to find out. You show respect for your customers not by leaving their needs unmet (as you may do if you take a hands-off approach), but by meeting them in ways that are comfortable for them. This means that you can approach this customer in a variety of ways.

However, few people in the world are completely at ease approaching strangers who enter a retail store: The ones who are good at it have usually received extensive training. Look for conferences and workshops that focus particularly on drawing customers out of their shells, not just on general sales training. By honing your skills in this area — and becoming someone with whom customers like interacting — you may be able to become far more comfortable doing something you used to think was impossible.

Acting as a maître d'

When people walk in, greet them warmly and welcome them to your fine store. Make them feel welcome, important, and delighted to have decided to visit you. You want your message to be, "Welcome, we're happy you're here, how can we help you?" How you say this depends on the customer in front of you. Some appreciate a direct question and respond positively; others prefer a greeting and the reassurance that's more like, "I'm right here if I can help you find anything."

The books you stock, the people you hire, and the atmosphere you create in your building are a part of this role (refer to Chapter 7 for more on creating ambiance). Your immediate goal when someone walks in is to make him comfortable. You don't do that by sitting behind the cash-wrap area and barely acknowledging his presence; you do that by finding the right words that make this person feel at ease and by creating a store that welcomes customers as you would welcome someone to your home.

Getting wrapped up in gift wrapping

One way to delight customers is by offering to wrap every book for free. This service fills a need because customers save the time and energy they would have spent wrapping their own gifts; but the service is good for you, as well, because it encourages customers to think of books as gifts.

Some booksellers spend a little extra money to stock thick, luxurious wrapping paper and beautiful ribbons. (Don't forget to place some lovely gift cards for sale at the cash-wrap area.) These stores train the staff to wrap well — no tape or seams showing — just like the best department stores do. This small service alone can make your shop stand out in customers' minds as a place that cares about them.

Acting as a problem-solver

Because of your connection to books — storehouses of information — you can help readers find information. Maybe that involves selling something, and maybe it doesn't, but don't worry too much about that. Be so approachable that customers tell you their need for information, and then set about fulfilling it.

One bookseller tells a story of a woman who called the shop and explained that she had heard a portion of a poem on the radio and wanted to hear the rest. She had called the radio station, but it wouldn't help her. So, she called the store and told the bookseller what she knew — a few lines of the poem. Although no sale was even possible, the bookseller found the poem and read it over the phone to the woman, who was absolutely gleeful. Think this woman is going to stop by the store the next time she wants to buy a book? Of course she is!

Some people call reference librarians for this type of information, because they know that the local library has trained professionals who will help them find the answers. Use your knowledge of books and your high-tech reference tools to position your store as an educational resource in your community.

You want to create an environment in which your customers call you because they know they can count on you to get their questions answered.

Suppose a customer comes in looking for information about a particular subject, and you locate a perfect book that you can special order and have in her hands in two days. She appreciates the information, but tells you she'll order it from Amazon.com herself. Do you kick her out the door and tell her never to come back?

No, you seize the educational opportunity — for you and your customer. Tell her she could help you make your business better by explaining why she prefers to order from Amazon than get the book from you. Listen to her answer and see whether you can discover anything. Don't argue with her or diminish her reasoning, but do let her know that you can get the book more quickly and remind her she won't pay postage if she orders through you.

Dan Chartand of Water Street Bookstore uses a technique of *racing* Amazon. He tells his customers that they are under no obligation to buy the book from him, but he'll order it anyway and notify them when it's in the shop. Then he scrambles to get the book within a day or two and calls to let the customer know that it's in. In some cases, the customer hasn't even been online to order a copy yet, and Dan saves the sale! When the customer has ordered the book already, Dan still makes an impression, because nine times out of ten, he can beat Amazon on delivery. The next time that customer wants a book, he or she is more likely to call Water Street Bookstore.

Acting as an expert

Customers count on you to know about books: That's precisely why they come to you. Read a lot — and encourage your staff to read and share their discoveries with you and other staff members. Use this pool of knowledge to build storewide confidence and expertise in recommending books to customers. Every book has to be a special, memorable, and favorable experience for your customers, so when you approach them, be a book expert, not a salesperson.

Acting as a psychic

By thinking about particular customers of yours as you read and evaluate new books, you have an opportunity to read their minds. When a customer comes in, you can say, "Do I have a book for you!" and put the book into the customer's hands. This process is called *handselling*, and it's a way to turn your customers on to books long before the media does. As you read, think of customers who may connect to that book and then seek that person out with a note or a phone call or by immediately reaching for that book the next time the customer comes in.

Going to the galleys

A *galley*, also known as an *advance reading copy* or *ARC,* is a prepublication version of a book that a publisher provides to booksellers, reviewers, and media outlets. For booksellers, a galley advance can be a critical tool in handselling a book. How? Well, galleys (which are often still being revised by the publisher and are in a rough stage), give you a chance to read the book before anyone else and be excited about the title the first day it can be sold. Before anyone else is talking about the book — and certainly before the book appears on talk shows — you've already been putting the book into the hands of certain customers and telling them how much they'll enjoy it.

Sales reps sometimes give you galleys; often, however, you have to not only ask, but *hound* the rep until you get a book's galleys. Galleys are limited in number, so you're fighting with others for the opportunity to review the book early. And, sometimes, if a rep tells you he honest-to-gosh doesn't have any galleys to give you for a particular book, he's probably telling the truth: Some books simply don't have galleys that are released to the public.

An alternative to reading galleys is to ask your rep for a review copy when you place the order. This way, you still receive a finished book to read or share with your staff, and sometimes, your review copy arrives a little bit ahead of publication. In the few days you gain between getting a review copy and waiting for your regular shipment to come in, you can read the book and begin handselling it to certain customers. Even if the review copy comes later, having an extra copy of the title means that you don't have to borrow from stock to read the book.

Have you seen Amazon.com's version of handselling? When you look at titles online, information pops up that tells you, "customers who bought this book also liked another book." After you buy a particular title, the next time you log on, you're told about several other titles in that category that you may enjoy. Amazon makes excellent recommendations a lot of the time, and they also offer customers the chance to read reviews by other readers. The power of this technological selling tool can't be underestimated.

Still, this electronic approach has a problem. Electronic handselling involves no personal knowledge of the customer. This approach reads a customer like a robot that follows a simple formula, and recommends books based solely on the category the publisher prints on the back cover. If you get to know your customers' tastes, and you ask the right questions, you can make your suggestions far more personal than any electronic system can.

Information about your customers' favorite authors, hobbies, career goals, religious affiliations, and so on, is gold. The more you can accumulate information about your customers' interests, the better you can anticipate their needs. If, for example, a customer likes a particular author, you can call or e-mail when that author's next book comes out. (Refer to Chapter 3 for more on gathering data from your customers.)

Acting as a tour guide

If your bookstore is located in a hot tourist area, become a community resource for tourists. Be the person who knows the best place to eat, fish, snorkel, ski, sunbathe, catch a movie, and so on. Although positioning yourself this way takes time, if you're willing to take time to help one customer with information that seems to have nothing to do with selling books, soon word will spread, and people will begin going to your store just to get the best advice about your geographic area. (And, as Chapter 8 tells you, getting customers in the door is the first step in selling books to them.) Heck, even locals may start asking you where the best prime rib in the city can be found.

Acting as a matchmaker

You're not matchmaking in a Yenta/*Fiddler on the Roof* sort of way, but in a social way. If a customer's unmet need is to interact and socialize, bring your customers together in social situations. Suggest that the customer participate in an upcoming event, book club, or writing group. If a discussion begins between you and one customer, see whether you can draw a second customer into that discussion (if this seems appropriate) so that the two of them begin talking, comparing notes — socializing! A bookstore doesn't have to be a library, in which everyone keeps their voices down, but can become a hub of literary and social discourse. Do you think Thoreau, Emerson, Alcott, Longfellow, Hawthorne — and occasionally, Dickens and Thackeray, visiting from England — gathered at the Old Corner Bookstore in Boston to quietly select a book, pay for it, and head home? Heck no! They went because they wanted to gather with other booklovers, who were also friends and colleagues. The Old Corner was a gathering place, not a buying place, although they bought, too.

Acting as a friend

If you're a person who likes to socialize, do so! Consider every person who walks through the door a potential friend, and don't worry about buying and selling. That will take care of itself.

One bookseller tells the story of a woman who had just been checked into a hospital and was told she'd be there for a few days. She called the bookstore to see whether a friend could pick up a few books for her to read while she passed the time. Rather than getting the friend involved, the bookseller hand-delivered a few choice books to the hospital that same day.

As you develop relationships with customers, begin to treat them as you do your other friends. If you know that a customer is struggling, send a card or note, just as you would do in a personal relationship.

Be sure that socializing is a need for each customer. If a customer is in a hurry, not in a social mood, naturally introverted, and so on, don't press. Make a social invitation through your words and demeanor, but don't be offended if a customer doesn't decide to be your friend at that moment.

Assuring Repeat Business

Getting customers in the door the first time isn't easy (although Chapter 8 is chock-full of ideas on how to do this). After you get customers in your store the first time, you need to do everything you can during that initial visit to get them to come back again and again. A key to developing a thriving bookshop is to build a base of loyal customers who wouldn't dream of shopping anywhere else, because they've built a relationship with you and your staff.

Customers come back because they've had a superior experience. They were surprised and delighted by what they found at your store. They liked it there, and they can see themselves becoming friends with you and your staff. Because of their joy in finding a place they didn't even know existed, they want to commit to doing business with you again.

If you blow the opportunity the first time a customer walks in your door, you've probably lost a customer forever. If you ignore a customer (or make a halfhearted attempt to connect but really just want to do your paperwork in the back room), don't attempt to get to know him, don't help problem-solve, and don't show a deep knowledge of and passion for your products, he won't be back. Oh, you may see him in your store again — especially if you're the only bookstore around and he needs a book quickly — but you won't have developed that person into a loyal customer who will buy his last book (both in terms of "the last book he has read" and "the last book in his life") from you.

If you're not getting a lot of repeat business — or if customers are coming in, taking a look around, and leaving — you may need to put yourself into your customer's shoes or take a little peek inside their brains. Here are some ideas:

  ✔ Once a month, take a stroll through your store and try to notice details, without thinking about how they came to be that way.

    • Is your front door dirty and worn?

    • Are your window displays stale?

    • What shape is your flooring in — is it threadbare?

- Are your paintings, posters, or other wall hangings out of date?

- Do your category signs look worn?

- Are your shelves dusty and bland?

- Is your cash-wrap crowded and fussy?

- What do your sidelines say about your store's mission?

- Are your merchandise bags chintzy-looking?

Be determined to see your store the way it really looks to customers. Be critical and act as if you're a customer seeing your store for the first time. You're awfully familiar with your store, so you have to force yourself to notice details that you may overlook every day.

Don't overlook the importance of training your staff to be as customer-friendly as you are. Although you want your customers to count on your personal recommendation, if they want the personal recommendation of a particular staff member, that's even better. You aren't always available, but you need to feel certain that the level of service on the sales floor is as good — or better — when you're in the office paying the bills.

✔ Develop a customer-response card that you hand out to select customers (see Figure 9-1). Ask these customers to fill out the survey and send it in or drop it in a special box just for that purpose. Offer to draw one survey out of the box in a week's time and give a $25 gift certificate to the name drawn.

If you print these reader-response cards on your laser printer, you can change them frequently to reflect whatever information you want at that time. If you've changed the look of one section of your store, ask customers about that. If you've started up a new category, see what they think. If you want to get their opinions on a new idea that you haven't launched yet, describe the idea and get some feedback.

✔ When you meet other independent booksellers at workshops or conferences, ask them to visit your store and be a secret shopper, arriving unannounced and behaving like a first-time customer but actually evaluating your physical space and customer service.

Archetype Books needs your help finding out about a new service
we're considering making available to you. May we take a few
minutes of your time to ask a few questions? If your response card is
drawn from the hat on Saturday, June 14, you'll win a $35 gift
certificate to the store.

Archetype Books is considering adding a café to our store. Would
knowing that you could enjoy a hot beverage or pastry affect how
often you visit our store?

☐ Yes, more likely to visit   ☐ Yes, less likely to visit

☐ No, doesn't matter

If we serve sandwiches and light snacks, will that affect your decision
to visit the store and café?

☐ Yes, more likely to visit   ☐ Yes, less likely to visit

☐ No, doesn't matter

Our goal is to make our café a pleasant and enjoyable experience. Can
you imagine coming downtown to visit our café even if you weren't
planning to visit our bookstore?

☐ Yes, likely to visit café   ☐ No, likely to visit only when
                                           visiting bookstore

What hours would be most convenient for you to visit Archetype Café?

☐ Same hours as bookstore   ☐ Earlier in AM   ☐ Later in PM

What beverages would you likely choose when visiting the café?
(Check all that apply.)

☐ Coffee   ☐ Tea   ☐ Hot chocolate   ☐ Smoothies

☐ Soy drinks   ☐ Iced drinks   ☐ Sodas   ☐ Wine   ☐ Beer

Do you see yourself using a café card that works like a debit card, but
can be used only at our café?

☐ Yes   ☐ No

Please feel free to make any suggestions in the space below. Thank
you for your time and your thoughts.

_____

_____

_____

_____

_____

_____

_____

_____

Figure 9-1: A sample customer-response card: Coffee
and books, anyone?

Taking Advantage of Additional Sales Opportunities

Many booksellers — especially those who manage the big, corporate superstores — focus on selling the books and sidelines that are sitting in the store right now (or can be quickly ordered through a distributor and arrive in a day or two). They also focus on selling them to the customers who walk in and take a look around or surf to the Web site.

However, bookselling is becoming less of a business that allows you to wait for customers to walk in the door and buy books off the shelf. Instead, you must be willing to market yourself outside the four walls of your establishment. You can create additional sales by looking beyond that standard model of bookselling, actively promoting special orders and going after institutional sales, as explained in the following two sections.

Special orders

A *special order* is a customer order that you place for a book that you don't have in stock. Some special orders are easy. They arrive in a day or two from a wholesaler. Other special orders may be for titles that must come directly from the publisher (which takes five to seven business days to arrive), involves shipping fees (which the customer sometimes picks up), and takes time to find and get to the store. Special orders aren't always profitable, because the discount from the publisher is often 20 percent (or even less) and the extra time and effort spent divert your attention from other tasks. However, special orders are extremely valuable to your business because you have an opportunity to meet a customer's needs in a way your competitors probably can't. That's why many independent bookstores do a lot of special ordering, and they do make money at it.

Some booksellers special order everything, even if the customer is noncommittal and they don't have any guarantee of a sale. Think of inquiries by customers as sales leads that you can follow up with a special order. You may even want to avoid the term "special order" completely, because it implies that you're going out of your way for the customer and expect a sale in return. When initiating a special order, you may say something like, "We don't have the book in stock right now, but we can have it for you on Friday. If you give me your information, I'll call you when it arrives." This approach is highly effective for books you're happy to stock, even if this particular sale falls through. Of course, if the title is highly technical or specialized and you're sure this is the only customer in your lifetime who'll want this book, you may want to get more of a commitment before you order the book.

A *STOP order* is a way that some publishers allow you to order one copy of the book and get the full discount. When placing special orders, always say that you're making a STOP order. The publisher may not be able to honor your request, but it's worth a try! Also ask how you can get the best discount on each order, for example, by using a credit card or by agreeing not to return the book.

Special orders: A real-life example

Filling a special order is like being a detective, figuring out where to look for a title while hunting it down. Last Christmas season, a good customer went into Book Ends in Winchester, Massachusetts, looking for a book called *Vinum: The Story of Roman Wine* for his son, who was doing a paper on wine for a high-school class. Students being as they are about deadlines, the dad (a great wine connoisseur himself) needed to get the book into his son's hands quickly. The title wasn't carried by wholesalers, and it wasn't even listed in any of the usual bookstore reference databases. Instead of assuming that the book was out of print or unavailable, the staff at Book Ends did more research. They discovered that the author was the publisher (Art Flair Publications) and that he lived in Pennsylvania. The manager called Information to get the number and soon reached the author, who was delighted to sell a copy to the bookstore.

The book arrived and was in the student's hands in time for him to write his paper. But the story of the special order doesn't end there. The dad was so impressed by the book that he returned a few days later and ordered 20 copies to give as Christmas presents — this was a hardcover book with a retail price of $38. That special order definitely earned its keep.

Customers often come into independent bookstores because they want to see something different, something eclectic, and not the standard bestsellers. Most customers understand that because your selection is unique, you can't carry everything, but they also expect you to know how to find books, get them fast, and let the customer know when they come in.

Institutional sales

Another opportunity for sales lies in *institutional sales;* that is, any bulk orders to businesses, schools, local government, conventions, festivals, and so on.

The key to capitalizing on institutional sales is twofold:

- ✔ You need to be fully connected to your community when you approach local businesses, school officials, and government officials, so that the institution feels as though it's turning to someone local and well known to fill its orders.

- ✔ Your store has to be staffed well enough to handle the extra effort you'll put into institutional sales. As the owner, if you pursue corporate sales with any vigor, before long, you won't have time to manage it and will probably have to hire someone to manage corporate sales for you. One way to justify hiring someone to handle this role is to also assign all offsite events (including bookfairs and offsite author visits) to this person.

Here's an example of how Boulder Book Store in Boulder, Colorado, not only immersed itself in institutional sales but started a sideline business, as well:

> David Bolduc, owner of Boulder Book Store, heard about a *Yoga Journal* conference of about 1,400 people that was scheduled a few months down the road in a nearby area. David approached the editor of the journal and asked whether he was interested in having Boulder Book Store start a bookstore at the conference. The editor agreed, and the bookstore was a great success. Now, Boulder Book Store runs bookstores at all four of *Yoga Journal's* conferences around the country (one is on a cruise ship!). The relationship hasn't stopped there,

however. As a result of running efficient bookstores at these conferences, the editor asked
David whether the store could also manage
the registration portion of the conferences for
them, registering participants, coordinating
with hotels, and so on, and that has grown into
a small but profitable side business that doesn't
take anything away from the bookstore. Given
that Boulder Book Store boasts one of the best
yoga sections in the country, both of these
extensions fit the store's original mission.

Boulder Book Store is now approaching other
groups to run bookstores at their conferences,
too. In addition, two national organizations are
located in the area, and they both do quite a bit
of training over the Internet, so the bookshop
may begin fulfilling their Internet book orders.

These types of institutional sales are profitable because they
have a captured group (at a conference or taking a class) that's
going to buy more books than other people would. They're
inspired by the conference going on around them. Conference
leaders and instructors can sign the books they've written,
and conference attendees can get the books they want!

Consider some additional ways that you can sell books to captive audiences:

- ✔ Get on a mailing list of conferences in your area, and then
  call the conference organizers to see whether you can
  open a bookstore during the conference. (Keep in mind
  that this is no small task: You have to free up some
  employees to work at the conference and transport the
  books and supplies, such as a cash register or two, to the
  conference.)

- ✔ Talk to a small university — especially one with a small
  or nonexistent bookstore — about supplying textbooks
  to the school. If a small college bookstore in your area
  sells textbooks but few other types of books, find out
  whether you can sell books during author appearances
  at the college.

- ✔ Work with local governments to determine whether you
  can supply books to any particular departments or for

training. You may be able to become an offsite bookstore for an entire government department or agency.

Note that multiple-copy sales to for-profit businesses have become difficult because of the availability of books in bulk directly from publishers and on the Internet. In order to supply a local business with books for internal use, you may have to offer a significant discount. You don't always have to match price, but you do have to offer a similar value for the business dollar. Your willingness to track down any title, recommend similar titles, and deliver the books personally translates into time savings for the business customer, and they, more than anyone, know that time is money.

✔ Contact local churches and synagogues to see whether they want to have a large presence of books on some aspect of faith. Or, if a church or synagogue sponsors author events, see whether you can support that event with books by the authors.

✔ Run book fairs *inside* your store. Book fairs are traditionally run at schools, but that approach can take too many employees out of your store. Instead, arrange for reps from the school (usually parents) to man special tables in your store, give out a card that indicates each book is part of the school book fair, and use your normal cash-wrap area to finalize the sale. The school gets a percentage of the sales (which you arrange with them ahead of time, preferably in a written contract), and you get two benefits: You establish a place in the community *and* you get an opportunity to show your store to new customers.

✔ Consider meeting with book clubs when they're setting up their reading schedules. You take along samples of several books that you think will meet their needs, and after they make their selections, book club members can come to your store and buy the books, perhaps even at a discount.

✔ If your town or other area organizes a local festival or contest each year, call the organizer and ask whether you can set up a table to supply books for it. You may not sell thousands of books about chili at the annual Five Alarm Chili Cookoff, but you'll be getting your name out into the community, and you're sure to sell quite a few books to this captive audience.

Chapter 10

Creating an Online Presence

- -

- -

*Y*our customers are online: doing research, looking at books, and even (gulp!) buying books online from other booksellers. Without your own Web site, you're essentially taking yourself out of the opportunity to get that book-buying business. In fact, because your customers do have to go elsewhere to buy their books online, they also see all sorts of other book-buying opportunities in the process, and those possibilities are eroding their customer loyalty. Give them an alternative — a Web site of your own!

In this chapter, you find out that getting your site up and running isn't prohibitively time-consuming, expensive, or high-tech, so you *can* throw your hat into the cyberspace arena. After all, the rewards of developing a site are boundless.

Unleashing the Power of a Bookshop Web Site

A Web site for your store is a powerful marketing tool that gives you the following paybacks:

- ✔ **Provides information:** Just as customers expect to see you in the Yellow Pages with at least a basic listing, they also expect to find you online. And, like your Yellow Pages choices — a regular listing, a full-page ad, or something in between — you get to decide how much of your marketing budget you want to invest in the site. At the very least, you want to establish a presence on the Internet that lets your customers know where you're located, how to reach you, and when your store is open.

  Even if your site is informational only (that is, customers can't check your inventory or place orders), you can provide a broad range of information. Check out any independent bookshop's Web site, and you find that the majority of the site is devoted to giving information (general info, staff recommendations, events, books clubs, and so on) and not to selling books.

- ✔ **Gives your customers flexibility:** You've built your business on providing the best possible service to your customers. So, by offering your customers the flexibility of the Internet — where they can get information and, potentially, order books 24/7 while wearing fuzzy pink pajamas — you make your Web site a big part of your service mix.

- ✔ **Eliminates your paper newsletter or catalog:** If you currently pay to print and mail newsletters or catalogs to your customers, you may be able to save yourself a bundle with a Web site that's combined with an e-mail newsletter. Many booksellers have converted their paper newsletters and catalogs to e-mail newsletters that liberally reference their Web sites and include links. Because few bookshops can afford to print paper catalogs in color, a Web site can actually be more attractive (with its color renderings of book jackets) for less money.

Selling books online

Your Web site is stronger as a marketing tool than as a sales tool, because much of the business generated by your Web site comes through your door or calls on the phone. Direct sales through the site are a smaller component, but are a component nonetheless. While many stores make their Web sites informational only, you fully realize the power of the Internet when you give customers the ability to buy books online. Even if you don't think buying books on the Internet is the best way for customers to purchase your products, you need to understand that people buy books online for any number of reasons:

✔ They don't think you'll have the book in stock and don't want to make an extra trip to the store — one to order a book and another to pick it up.

✔ They may not have much time and want books waiting for them when they drop by the store.

✔ They may enjoy the solitude of browsing your bookstore by themselves, going virtually from section to section to see what's available, without anyone interrupting that time.

✔ They may be homebound and need books to be delivered without a trip out of the house. Alternatively, they may be office-bound and so busy with work and life that they just don't have time to stop by the store in person.

✔ They may work nontraditional hours and need to visit your store during those four hours per night that you actually get some sleep!

✔ They may just prefer to shop online. That's right. Some folks enjoy the online experience more than a trip to the store. They may be younger, more technologically savvy, or just more connected to technology. Before you say, "That isn't *my* customer," stop to think about your bookstore's future and the new customers you'll need to attract and serve to be in business five, ten, or twenty years from now.

Be sure to include a place on your site where customers can sign up for your e-mail newsletter. In addition, encourage store customers to provide an e-mail address and opt-in to the Internet mailing list.

✔ **Promotes store events:** The primary reason you develop a Web site is to bring customers into your store, and one way to do this is to make a big splash on your *home page* (the first page customers see when they log on to your site) about events. Although you also want to promote events in the store, your Web site can tell customers who's coming to visit and list full bios, synopses and/or reviews of books, pictures of jacket covers, and so on. You can also give full details about each event, including dates, times, and locations.

Consider e-mailing a reminder about events one or two days before they take place. The e-mails themselves can be short, with a link to the Web page. The Alabama Booksmith in Birmingham, Alabama, for example, sends a short e-mail to over 4,000 customers just before each event that lists the event, date, and time, and then says "see the Web site for details." The store's site then includes all of the details about the event, author, and so on.

Developing a Cool Web Site

What makes a great Web site? Consider the following elements that booksellers around the country frequently include in their exemplary sites:

✔ **Events:** Events (discussed in Chapter 8) draw customers to your store, so make sure every event is front and center on your Web site. While not every customer wants to attend every event, customers are frustrated when they miss an author appearance or other event that would have appealed to them. A great Web site makes event information easy to communicate.

✔ **Staff reviews and recommendations:** Your customers love seeing staff recommendations in the store and reading staff reviews in your newsletter, and they make your Web site shine, too. The same elements that make your independent bookstore great — reviews, staff favorites, personal (sometimes passionate) assessments, and dialogue about books — can also make your Web site stand out.

✔ **New local books (semi-monthly or monthly):** Local books are an opportunity to make your site substantially different from Internet-only bookstores, and they traditionally are a big hit with local customers. Showcase local books on your site, and you'll quickly build customer loyalty.

✔ **Book club updates:** Both in-store book clubs and any book club that orders through your store can have its own page that lists current and upcoming selections, meeting dates and locations, and any other relevant information.

✔ **Great customer service:** Plenty of online customers are frustrated, and you have a chance to meet their needs through your site. Encourage customers to e-mail you if they're not finding what they need: Via e-mail, you can research and find books for them (just as you do for your in-store customers), suggest alternatives when a book truly isn't available, and find other personal ways to serve online customers.

Make sure that you keep up with your e-mail and remember that life moves at a faster pace in the virtual world.

✔ **Unique flavor:** Most of all, great bookshop sites don't try to be just another Web site. Use your site to be yourself, letting your store's unique personality shine through. Make sure that your headings are unique to the store — see Figure 10-1 for a look at The Regulator Bookshop's (Durham, North Carolina) home page, which invites customers to order a book, pick it up, and have lunch in The Regulator's café. Your special touches and personalization make your customers want to come back for more.

Figure 10-1: Where else can you pick up a book — and lunch?

Recognizing the Drawbacks

Web sites aren't perfect — they're close, though! Getting a Web site up and running takes two resources that may be limited:

- **Money:** Setting up a site with BookSense.com (see the following section) carries a one-time cost of about $350 and a monthly fee of $175 to $200 for a basic site from which customers can order books. As with anything, bells and whistles cost a little more, but you can pick and choose what you need. Sites that don't originate with BookSense.com may cost more or less, depending on the sorts of tools they offer and what kind of volume (also called *hits*) you expect.

  Your site may not generate enough sales to cover the entire cost (although many do), but it will probably come close. Keep in mind that if you market your site well, it can generate tremendous sales for your store. However, not all sales from your Web site come through as Web site sales — many customers will see your site, check your inventory, and then come in to buy the book.

  You may also be able to get newsletter co-op money (refer to Chapter 5) that helps pay for all or part of your site. For example, suppose your store features Staff Favorites in a prominent area or with special tags on the books. On your Web site, you can describe the Staff Favorites and include a staff review (as opposed to standard copy that may come from the publisher) for each book. By posting reviews online and displaying staff favorites in your store, you may be able to get co-op money from each publisher in the same way you would get it for a printed newsletter. How much co-op you get depends on how much you order of a particular title, in a season, or in the preceding year, and also depends on how much the publisher determines a Web site listing is worth. If you can keep your co-op request under $100 per listing, you'll have a better chance of getting approval from publishers. Using this approach, you can probably run your site for free or even for a profit. The co-op money isn't a freebie — after all, the staff has to read numerous books and write reviews for the ones they select — but chances are, they're doing that already.

- **Time:** The majority of the time you spend on a Web site is in the planning and initial set-up. After you think through your vision of the site and plan how to achieve that vision (and *you* should do that, even if you delegate the upkeep to someone else), getting a BookSense.com site up and running (see the following section) takes less than 12 hours. If you don't opt for a Booksense.com site, hire someone's teenage daughter to do the HTML coding for you, but be sure you still retain control of the site's overall look and feel.

HTML is short for *hypertext markup language,* a programming language used to design Web sites. Before you run for cover at the term "programming language," keep in mind that HTML is about the simplest computer language ever developed. If you can follow a recipe or instructions for how to program your VCR, you've already completed tasks that are more difficult than using HTML.

After the initial time investment, you or someone on your staff needs to spend time keeping the site fresh and interesting (and letting customers know that it's there — see the "Marketing Your Site" section, later in this chapter). In two to four hours a week, however, you should be able to do the following maintenance:

- **Check for orders (daily):** This activity is critical if you run a Web site that allows customers to place orders. If you check your orders daily and have the book in stock, you get to call customers the day of or day after they place orders and say — "voilá!, your book is in" (or, perhaps, skip the "voilá!"). If you don't have the book in stock and check for Web site orders in time to include those books in your wholesale order(s), you may be able to have the book at the store the next day, which is far better than any Internet-only bookseller can deliver.

- **Respond to customer e-mail (daily or twice-daily):** Answering e-mail questions promptly is the virtual equivalent of waiting on the customer in front of you. If you can't check e-mail at least once a day, assign this task to a staff member.

- **Post new events and delete ones that have passed (daily or weekly):** Nothing dates a Web site more than two-week-old events. Take events down the day after you hold them and post events far enough in advance to allow customers to plan their schedules around it.

- **Update staff recommendations and local books (weekly, semimonthly, or monthly):** If you date your staff recommendation (for example, "February Staff Favorites"), be sure that you change those dates the first of each month. Even if you don't date your recommendations, keep them fresh, so that customers frequently see something new when they log on.

- **Update book club selections (semimonthly or monthly):** You want your site to be the most convenient and most up-to-date way for book club members to get information, so keep adding to the book club selections and deleting books already read by the group.

- **Choose the Book Sense 76 titles that you want to feature on your site (bimonthly):** Refer to Chapter 8.

Do you need software to set up your Web page?

If you develop a site linked to BookSense.com (see the "Making Sense of BookSense.com" section, later in this chapter), you really don't need any other software, because you're given design tools that allow you to create the site you want. Although you don't have to be an HTML pro to set up your BookSense.com site, using some basic HTML for boldface and other formatting will make your site more visually appealing. The process is easier then you may think, and BookSense.com helps you out! If you go the BookSense.com route, you don't need to hire a *Webmaster* (roughly defined as a computer genius who designs and maintains your site, usually demands a pretty hefty salary, and as a group

has an average age of 15 years old). Instead, you can design and maintain an effective Web site on your own.

However, some bookshops choose not to integrate with BookSense.com. Some stores started their own sites before BookSense.com came online and decided not to switch over. A few others have taken their own Web sites and integrated the BookSense.com database and shopping cart into the back end of the process. If you decide to create your own site, you'll probably need to get your hands on FrontPage or any other sort of Web-page design software. Web-design software isn't rocket science, but you'll want to allow some time to master it before you begin designing your site.

Making Sense of BookSense.com

The main purpose of ABA's BookSense.com, the Internet arm of Book Sense (refer to Chapter 8), is to provide members of the Book Sense program with Web sites of their own, where members can market their stores and their products. Although you can always set up a site that's independent, by joining forces with BookSense.com, you realize the following benefits:

- ✔ **Tools that allow you to create a Web site on the BookSense.com server:** By setting up a BookSense.com site, you don't need any other special software or tools at your disposal — or any special technical knowledge, except some level of comfort with computers, including the one that tracks your inventory. The BookSense.com system is easy, and you can be up and running in less than a dozen hours.

- ✔ **Fresh content:** BookSense.com helps you keep your site fresh and lively. You can, for example, take advantage of the daily author birthday or daily quote about books. You can also take advantage of prepackaged news features and recommended reading each week.

- ✔ **Title database of over 2 million books:** By tapping into Ingram's database, which includes pictures of the jacket cover and descriptions of the book, your customers can check to see what titles you can deliver to them.

- ✔ **Orders filled from your store's stock:** BookSense.com can help you set up your site such that it shows *your* inventory, so that readers can check to see what's available in your store. If you choose to upload your own inventory to your BookSense.com site, you can also elect to be the first to fulfill customers' Web-based orders. Your customers can opt to order online and pick up their books at the store, or you can ship or hand-deliver books to customers from your own backroom.

- ✔ **Orders filled without your intervention.** If you prefer, you can elect to have Ingram or Baker & Taylor (refer to Chapter 5) fulfill some customer orders for you. These orders appear to come from you: Your store's name is on the outside of the carton and at the top of the packing list, as well. If Ingram or Baker & Taylor don't stock the book or are temporarily out of stock, the order is referred automatically to your store. For most stores, one in five orders

> is fulfilled directly by Ingram or Baker & Taylor — a number that's likely to rise in the coming years.
>
> ✔ **Access to the Book Sense 76:** Book Sense has been extremely successful in marketing the Book Sense 76 (refer to Chapter 8), and you can tap into this success by highlighting all or part of that list every other month. Of course, you can highlight any books you want — not just those on the Book Sense 76 — including local authors and other books of interest to your customers.

Marketing Your Site

After your site is up and running, people will come, right? The truth is, they won't — not unless you tell them that your site is there. Oh sure, maybe once or twice a year, someone halfway across the country will visit your site as the result of an Internet search. (Most booksellers report absolutely no sales from searches from around the globe that land people at their sites.) So, rather than waiting for people to come to you, you need to boldly announce to your customers that you have a great Web site just for them. How do you do this? Consider the following:

> ✔ **Put your *URL* (universal resource locator; aka your Web address) on everything that has your store name on it:** bags, bookmarks, business cards — you name it. Everywhere you put your store name, put your URL.
>
> ✔ **Place the URL on events' schedules and on all of your store's signage.** Some stores hang "as seen on the Web site" signs on Staff Recommended shelves, Book Sense 76 selections, and so on.
>
> ✔ **When you first launch your site, take out a newspaper ad announcing your site.** With any future ads, even ones that appear to have nothing to do with your Web site, always include your URL.
>
> ✔ **Announce a special, one-time-only Web site deal.** When customers check out with their purchases, give them a coupon for a discount on a Web site purchase (with a deadline one or two weeks in the future). At that time, ask for an e-mail address and approval to send the store's e-mail newsletter.

Consider holding periodic lotteries for customers who place an order through the site. Anyone who orders a book is entered into a lottery for a $100 gift certificate, a signed book, or other great prizes. You encourage Web site orders and also get customers into the store.

✔ **Develop an affiliate program:** When you launch an *affiliate program,* authors, chambers of commerce, kennel clubs, and anyone else with a Web site that promotes books can link to your site. You then fulfill the order and send the book(s) directly to the customer, giving the author or other organization a small fee (typically 2 to 6 percent of the wholesale price) for referring customers to your site. BookSense.com has an option for setting up this type of program.

St. Helen's Book Shop in St. Helens, Oregon, employs an extremely successful affiliate program. For more information on affiliate programs, see the St. Helen's Web site at `www.sthelensbookshop.com` and click on Become an Affiliate.

✔ **Equip your store with a computer *kiosk* (fancy word for booth or stall) that always has your site up and running.** Because you have the option of putting your store's inventory on your Web site, customers can use a computer kiosk to check the store's inventory; that is, they can find out that certain books are in the store without having to ask a bookseller (and keep in mind that some people — especially those who have grown up with computers and the Internet — prefer this way of interacting).

Make sure the kiosk is housed in a stand-up fixture so that customers don't sit down to surf the Net.

Training your employees to be comfortable with the Web site and to recommend it to your customers is critical to the site's success. To train your employees, have each employee place an order and then describe the experience — good and bad. You want everyone on your staff to be invested in the site, so that customers who come in the store hear about it.

Shipping and Delivering Goods

This chapter saves the best for last, because shipping and delivering books is the easiest part of running a store Web site. After all, fulfilling orders is what you do all day long. Keep in mind that customers usually receive books they order in the following ways:

- ✔ **Pick them up in the store.** This scenario is ideal for you, because customers come in to your store. It's also great for them, because they know that when they get to your store, the books they want will be off the shelves and waiting for them. No one pays any additional money for shipping, which means that you can be competitive with Amazon.com and other large online booksellers.

- ✔ **Have them delivered (if customers live within your geographic area).** If you're already doing this and have a process in place for delivering books within a small geographic area, operating a Web site and making this feature available will be no sweat.

If you don't currently deliver in your local area, don't offer this on your Web site unless you're prepared to take on the extra cost of this service (after all, someone has to physically leave your store and make the delivery, and that time spent costs you money). Instead, simply ship books within your geographic area the same way you would if you shipped outside the area — and charge for it the same way, too! (Consider offering a flat shipping charge based either on the dollars ordered or the number of books purchased rather than trying to calculate charges based on weight.) Internet customers are accustomed to being charged for shipping costs, although the lower you can keep the costs, the better. Amazon.com has had recent success with free shipping on orders over $25, so if you can offer free delivery and still make a profit, try doing so on larger orders.

- ✔ **Have them shipped (if customers are outside of your geographic area).** Chances are, you're already doing at least some shipping outside your area. If not, talk to your UPS or FedEx Ground carrier to set up an account. If you become a UPS or FedEx Ground customer, your carrier may be able to pick up your shipments to Web site customers when making deliveries to you. Having regular UPS or FedEx pick-up is also handy for other outgoing shipments — returns, for example (refer to Chapter 6).

When you first start shipping, use plain cardboard boxes with a bright label that includes your bookshop's name, address, phone number, and URL. Another way to draw

attention to a plain box is to have packing tape printed
with your store's name and URL. As you increase in
volume, consider buying cardboard boxes in a few different sizes with your store's name, logo, and URL preprinted
on the sides of the box.

✔ **Have them shipped next-day.** Occasionally, customers
need books sent via next-day delivery. Fed Ex Express is
usually your best bet for this service, and you can set up
an account for free. Fed Ex Express provides bags and
boxes for shipping (which means you don't have to provide your own box) and offers plenty of options for getting
the packages to your FedEx driver — the driver can pick
up in your store, or you can drop your package into a
FedEx pick-up box. Drop boxes are usually conveniently
placed — maybe one is close to your store. Pick-up times
vary by location, but they're usually around 5:00 p.m.

Starting on Thanksgiving, post a cut-off date for Christmas
delivery on your Web site. Make sure this information is in
big, bold letters, and make the date one you're sure that you
can keep. (Be sure to keep in mind that FedEx may pick up
early on Christmas Eve and New Year's Eve and don't deliver
on either of those two holidays.) Your date may need to be
earlier than that of large, Internet-based bookstores, because
if you miss a delivery, you have to look that customer right in
the eye and explain why Kaitlin's soccer book won't be under
the tree.

Part IV
Running an Efficient Small Business

The 5th Wave   By Rich Tennant

SCREW-U
Screws 'n Screwdrivers
CUSTOMER SERVICE

Screw-U! How can I... Hello? Dang!

Another, hang up Dave? Just a tip—next time try answering with a smile on your face.

In this part . . .

You find out how booksellers define their "ideal" employees, interview effectively to find them, and offer meaningful (and sometimes inexpensive) benefits. You get a glimpse at how to train your employees, delegate responsibility, and evaluate performance, as well.

You also find out how to manage your dreaded paperwork: taxes and important financial statements that can help you better manage your business.

Chapter 11

Hiring and Retaining Employees

· ·

In This Chapter

▶ Dreaming of the perfect employee

▶ Getting employees to view bookselling as a profession

▶ Figuring out who does what at your bookshop

▶ Training employees from the first day

▶ Giving frequent feedback

· ·

*I*f you got into bookselling because you wanted to surround yourself with good books and interact with likeminded, book-loving customers, you may consider managing employees — the interviewing, the paperwork (see Chapter 12), the training, and the evaluations — to be the most difficult aspects of your business. However, you don't have to loathe hiring and retaining employees.

Instead, good employees — think of them as good *bookselling partners* — can be the reason you love going to work every day. If you're savvy about how and when to invite employees to hone their craft in your store, how to convey your mission and vision for the store (refer to Chapter 2), how to share ownership with your employees, and how to keep your employees' long-term career goals in sight at all times, your bookshop can grow and thrive along with these associates who love books — and bookselling — as much as you do.

Describing the Ideal Employee

Booksellers around the country describe their ideal employees as people who not only love books, but who also thoroughly enjoy putting the right books into each customer's hands. Ideal employees keep their antennas finely tuned to your customers by remembering their names and tastes and welcoming them into the store as if it were the employee's own living room.

Ideal employees are eager to anticipate and meet your customers' needs and to be gracious as they go about meeting those needs. Customers feel comfortable and respected when they're interacting with ideal employees. Similarly, co-workers trust and enjoy working with ideal employees, who pitch in when needed and never feel that any task is beneath them.

Finding Mr. or Ms. Right

You may be saying, "sure, that's a great description of the ideal employee, but that person doesn't seem real." How do you pay $6 or $7 an hour and find someone who does all that? How do you keep employees from leaving as soon as a better-paying job comes along, forcing you to hire and train someone all over again?

Putting yourself in your employee's shoes

Start by putting yourself in your employee's shoes. If you didn't own or manage your bookshop and you were offered a position that included standing on your feet for several hours a day, working evenings and weekends, completing tasks that sometimes seemed menial, and doing it all at or just above the minimum wage, would you do it?

What if the store offered few benefits, less than you could get working at a local manufacturing plant (which probably pays more, as well) or even at the local Wal-Mart? Would you work at your store then?

What if you had a degree in English, the classics, comparative literature, or history? Would you stay long-term or would you work at the bookshop for a while and then leave when something more directly related to your field came along?

Until you can honestly say that under those conditions, you'd work at the bookstore and plan to stay for the rest of your career, few of the people you interview will meet your vision of an ideal employee.

Making bookselling a viable career option

Many people want to make a career out of bookselling, not in their own stores but in your store and in others like it. They want to share their love of books, get to know customers and find out how to meet their needs, cheerfully complete even the most menial of tasks (as long as it has to do with their beloved books!), and treat co-workers with kindness and respect.

Unfortunately, among the many who want to make a career of bookselling, few do. Too many Americans define success as working at a day job that's directly related to their college degrees, Monday through Friday, for a wage that allows them to buy a house, drive a nice car, and invest in retirement funds. That's what you're competing with, not with the clothing store next door that offers 25 cents an hour less than you do.

Unlike many other retail operations that expect heavy turnover, you have to find a way to make bookselling a viable, long-term career option for each of your highly skilled, well-educated, well-read employees, whether you hire one part-timer who comes in two nights a week or 200 full-time employees at your humongous bookshop.

Suppose you're employing a student at the local college who's majoring in English and works part time at your store. He's a terrific employee, connects with your customers, reads industry magazines and Web sites during his break, and gobbles up book after book in his spare time. When he graduates, you assume he'll leave the store and get a job in editing, writing, or teaching, or go on to grad school.

How do you get this employee to stay on, permanently? Here are some starting points:

✔ **Start talking to him now about making bookselling his career.** Ask about his post-collegiate career goals and ask what you can do to put bookselling on his list of top-five options. Be honest, however, about his potential career path and promotions in the coming years, especially if your bookshop is quite small.

Bookselling is too often a fall-back plan for liberal arts majors who aren't hired for their dream jobs. Don't let your bookshop accept this second-class status. Bookselling is a dream career, too, and one that should accept only individuals who are serious about committing to it for the long haul.

✔ **Find out what interests him so much about editing, writing, teaching, or the other career options he's considering.** See whether any of those needs can be met in your store, such as writing or editing a newsletter or catalog, or giving monthly seminars as part of an ongoing event at your store, and so on. If public relations interests him, decide whether he can work into a leading role in promoting store events. If he's a natural at merchandising, see whether you can include managing displays as a part of his training and (eventually) as a part of his full-time responsibilities.

✔ **See whether he can take elective classes that will serve him well in the bookselling business.** Can he take a class in merchandising? Sales and marketing? Public relations? Retail management? Inventory control? Help him plan for a career in bookselling while he's still in school, just as he would do for another dream job.

✔ **Research the starting salary for graduates in his field and determine whether you can compete with it.** Starting salaries for liberal arts majors usually aren't so high that you couldn't come close to matching it.

✔ **Find out his ideal working schedule.** Perhaps he has always been a night person and dreads the thought of working nine to five for the rest of his life. If he can work noon to eight, five days a week, he may be more satisfied than he would be elsewhere. If you're located in a resort town that has downtime for certain months of the year, find out whether taking the winter or summer off would mesh with his lifestyle.

✔ **Determine what benefits his other job options may offer.** Crunch the numbers and see what's the best benefits package you can provide him and your other employees.

✔ **Sell him on the unique benefits of bookselling:** being on the cutting edge of the publishing business, meeting authors, affecting book-buying decisions, introducing customers to the world and life of books, and defending the First Amendment.

Offering meaningful benefits

When you utter the word *benefits,* most people think of medical insurance, 401(k) plans, and maternity leave. And yes, those benefits are of critical importance to employees who have no other medical coverage, who don't see how they'll ever be able to retire on their current salaries, and who'd like to raise a family while building a career at your store. Ideally, your store offers these sorts of benefits. If you think about it, most of the other jobs that your employees would likely consider are not at other retail venues with slim benefit packages, but at corporations that require their intelligence and educational backgrounds *and* offer the benefits to match.

Don't be too quick to dismiss insurance and/or personal leave as something you can't possibly afford to offer your staff. Meet with a trusted insurance agent and/or financial consultant to determine whether you can afford these options, many of which practically guarantee long-term employment among your staff. Independent bookstores around the country have found ways to offer paid medical and dental insurance with a reasonable deductible, life and disability insurance, 37.5-hour work weeks for salaried employees, several weeks of paid vacation and personal time, paid maternity leave, low-cost bus passes, 401(k) plans (both with and without matching funds), annual or semiannual bonuses, and so on. These benefits may even be available for part-time employees.

Turning convention on its ear: Encouraging short-term employment

A dozen years ago, when jobs were plentiful and booksellers were having trouble hanging on to their best employees, bookstore consultant Kate Whouley wrote an article that argued against trying to "keep" good employees. Although the market has changed today, Kate's premise still rings true for a smaller bookshop, where you may not be able to create a dream job when your ideal student employee graduates from college. Rather than settling for average employees who may stick around indefinitely, hire great people, teach them all you know, and encourage them to move onward and upward in the business — even if that means they move out of your store. When you encourage your employees to improve all the skills they can, they will be challenged and productive for as long as they're with you. When they're ready to move on, applaud their efforts and help them out — whether they want to become publishers' sales reps, open bookstores of their own, or apply to MFA programs. You'll not only get the satisfaction of seeing your protégés move up in the world, but your store will gain the reputation as a great place to begin a career in the book business.

Be sure to think beyond the standard definition of "benefits," for example:

- ✔ What sort of book discount can you offer your employees? Can they get books at cost?
- ✔ Can friends and relatives receive a discount?
- ✔ Can your employees borrow books from the store and never have to spend money on books at all?
- ✔ Can they get free advance copies or bound galleys from sales reps (refer to Chapter 6)?
- ✔ Can they attend regional or national conferences or ABA Booksellers School?
- ✔ Can they have their own desks or small offices?

✔ Can you provide each employee with business cards and a private phone extension, voice mailbox, and/or e-mail address?

✔ Can you provide each employee with a key to the store? (Don't think you can? Keep in mind that every one of the nearly 200 employees at Denver's Tattered Cover Book Store receive a key to the store on their first day of work.)

✔ Can every employee sign for merchandise or even sign for the store credit card?

✔ Can you offer flexible schedules that are realistic in their lives? Or, on the flip side, can you give daytime, business-week hours to someone who's married to a daytime employee?

Before you say "no" to any of these options, keep in mind that other independent bookstores of varying sizes throughout the nation offer at least some of these benefits to their employees.

Interviewing effectively

Happily, many booksellers don't have to go looking for employees. Instead, potential employees, especially part-time candidates — booklovers of all stripes and sizes — come to you, résumé in hand.

Even if you don't have to advertise for employees, you do need to identify those individuals who will mesh with your store and those who won't. Here are some tips for using interviews to sift through the available applicants and find employees who will devote themselves to your bookshop.

✔ **Look for personable individuals** who live in the community (or have just moved in) and love books.

✔ **Start evaluating a prospective employee the moment he asks for an application.** If you meet the potential applicant, observe him closely. How well does he interact with your bookselling staff? How does he present himself on the day he applies? Is he tuned in to the fact that it's a busy day? If you don't meet the applicant yourself, encourage your staff members to pass their observations to you along with the application.

✔ **Discuss the shop's mission and vision** (refer to Chapter 2) and look for responses in the form of facial expressions and body language during the interview.

✔ **Ask challenging questions and carefully evaluate responses.** Make your questions practical and specific. For example, ask potential employees to discuss problems they encountered in a recent job and how they solved them. If they say there were no problems, dig deeper.

✔ **Let the applicant speak.** Too many managers and owners make the common mistake of talking too much in an interview. Yes, you want to share some information about the store and your expectations for a potential staff member, but the purpose of an interview is to screen the applicant based on what he has to say.

✔ **Evaluate how well a potential employee articulates.** The Catch-22 of hiring employees is that a lot of people who love books aren't that comfortable working with people.

✔ **Before you interview, draft a list of questions you want to ask each applicant.** This list helps you stay on course and gives you a chance to hear a few different answers to the same question. But don't get so hung up on your list of questions that you forget to listen to the answers. The best question you ask may not be on your list, because it's based on an applicant's response to another question. Don't let the interview go too far off on a tangent, but give yourself and the applicant some flexibility.

✔ **When you give information to the applicant, pay attention to how well a potential employee listens.** Is he tuned in to you? Is he comfortable with silence and not always giving the quick answer?

✔ **Ask about comfort with technology.** Most cash registers and inventory management systems are computerized, so an employee who's afraid of computers may not ever feel at home in your store.

✔ **Discuss the job realistically.** Don't sugar-coat the difficult aspects of the job, or employees will quit after a few weeks.

✔ **Talk about long-term commitments.** Tell potential employees that you're hiring people for the long haul.

Dividing the Pie: Sharing Responsibilities

At most small (and many large) independent bookstores, all employees perform many different functions: opening and closing the store, running the cash register, receiving, shelving, counting inventory, cleaning, and taking special orders.

More specialized tasks tend to include setting up displays, buying frontlist titles (although at many stores, all employees have input), buying sidelines, buying children's books, reordering, dealing with incorrect orders or damaged books, and coordinating returns. Still, these tasks aren't so specialized that you couldn't train all of your employees to manage some of all of them, too. If you want your employees to feel they're a part of your team, train them on as many jobs as possible.

Deciding whether to hire a manager

How does the owner of a small bookshop decide whether it's time to hire a manager? Consider the following situations:

✓ You're pooped from too much work. If you're consistently getting less than eight hours of sleep, are at the store six or seven days every week, and don't have a life outside the store, you'll soon get sick or lose interest in your shop.

✓ You see a simple way to split your responsibilities, for example, you can hire someone to manage the children's section while you continue frontlist buying for adult books, or you hire someone to manage the day-to-day operations while you manage events and other PR work.

✓ You recognize that you're completing tasks that you're not especially skilled at. If you're not great at managing employees but could hire a manager or supervisor who is, you can focus on the tasks at which you excel.

✓ You're thinking of retiring in the next five or ten years and would like to groom someone to take over.

✓ You're thinking of expanding to another location or pursuing another business venture (such as a small publishing company) and need someone to manage the store in your absence.

If you'd like your employees to have more input into the frontlist buying process, ask your sales reps (refer to Chapter 5) to give a seasonal preview and talk to the entire store. Reps may be willing to come early to give an hour-long preview before you sit down to *work the buy* (decide which frontlist titles to order). Or, sometimes the sales reps will come to a store meeting and share their favorites from the season's list.

If you find that you and your staff are too busy at times to deal with certain important tasks, consider hiring freelancers on a project basis to take up some of the load:

✔ McLean & Eakin Bookshop in Petoskey, Michigan, hires a freelancer to produce its window displays. Every three weeks, he spends a day or two creating displays that no employee in the store can rival.

✔ Paz & Associates creates a national newsletter for booksellers that you can customize with schedules of events, an owner's column, reviews of local books, and so on. You can usually customize two or three of the eight pages.

✔ Freelance your Web site and catalog content. Nearly every area of the country boasts a local writer or editor whom you can employ for these short-term projects.

✔ Run portions of your store as independent businesses, with self-employed owners running those services. The services may include a café or coffee shop, a custom stationery shop, and a copy center/shipping counter.

Training Your Employees

Every new employee requires training, but the method of training varies greatly from bookshop to bookshop. At larger bookshops, for example, new employees often go through an established process and train in small groups with others just starting out. Smaller bookshops may ask a new employee to shadow or observe other employees. The training may vary from a breaking-in period in which the work isn't too difficult to intensive training that may be more difficult than the day-to-day job!

Some booksellers start new employees on the cash register. The idea is that by starting with customers from the first day, new employees won't fear that contact. Employees will also get used to the point-of-sale (POS) system and become comfortable with all the procedures at the cash-wrap area. Other bookstores start new employees in the receiving area, so that they get a feel for the store from the backroom first, and then move into shelving books to get comfortable with the inventory before coming into contact with real, live customers.

Although most booksellers attend regional and national book conferences and shows, these trips are usually reserved for buyers and PR/marketing people. If the event offers seminars, supervisors and managers may also attend. A great way to make new employees feel a part of your shop's team is to send them to BEA or the regional conferences. They'll understand more about the book biz from one day at a major book conference than they will from months on the job.

Even though new employees aren't doing your frontlist buying, you can still expose them to the process by having them shadow you as you order. You can do the same with every area or department in the store, so that every employee understands how his or her actions affect the jobs of others.

Staff meetings may seem like social time, but it's really training time. When your employees engage in frequent, lively discussions (facilitated by you or your manager) about what books and events are coming up, what's going on in the store, what works and what doesn't, your new employees learn at the knees of your experienced employees.

Evaluating Performance

Many booksellers pale at questions about performance evaluations, so if you're cringing as you read this section, you're not alone.

Evaluating performance isn't an easy task for anyone, so nearly everyone — from bookshop owners to corporate executives — minimizes the headache by giving a fairly nonspecific evaluation after the first 30 or 90 days (something along the lines of, "You're doing a fine job — do you have any questions or concerns?") and then following that one up with annual reviews.

But consider this: Suppose your spouse or significant other does something that really bugs you nearly every day of the year. Rather than talking about this behavior early on — say, the second or third time it happens — you wait an entire year, putting notes into a file each time you catch him or her doing the dirty deed. At the end of that frustrating year, in which you constantly bit your tongue, you whip out the file, reveal your list of evidence, and then finish up with a triumphant "gotcha." That's not a healthy relationship, yet it's exactly what managers around the country do to their employees every day of their business lives. Even if your feedback is positive rather than negative, would you wait an entire year to tell your spouse that dinner on February 9 was especially tasty or that the yard was nicely mowed last July 23? Of course not!

Don't think of performance evaluations as annual events; think of them as everyday opportunities to offer feedback, both positive and negative. Keep track of the feedback you give, but dispense with the formal, "it's time for your review" approach. Performance doesn't improve when you wait to give feedback or create a gotcha situation at the end of the year in which you list all of your employees' misdemeanors. Instead, catch employees doing great work and give them positive feedback. When you see an employee doing something that bothers you, deal with the issue right away, giving feedback on the wrong behavior, not on the individual as a person. For more on giving ongoing positive and negative feedback, check out *Coaching & Mentoring Employees For Dummies* by Marty Brounstein (Wiley Publishing, Inc.).

If an employee's performance is consistently poor, and you've given ongoing feedback, establish a date by which the performance must improve to avoid termination. Always give fair warning and plenty of opportunity to improve, and put everything in writing, with dates and signatures by both you and the employee.

Several times a year, spend time with your employees to talk about their goals and careers. Go out to lunch and focus the entire conversation on where this employee sees him- or herself in the future. Find out which tasks appeal to each employee and spend time trying to find a niche for everyone. If you want your employees to spend their careers with you, their careers and long-term goals have to be your responsibility, too. Encourage your employees to be completely honest with you, even if their goals don't seem to mesh with yours. With a little creativity, you can probably find a way for even budding rocket scientists to find a long-term home at your store.

Chapter 12

Paying the Tax Man

● ●

In This Chapter

▶ Reviewing taxes on what you sell and what you store

▶ Looking at employee-related taxes

▶ Paying tax on that little bit of money you call a "profit"

● ●

*I*f you're like many booksellers, you not only know that death and taxes make up life's two inevitabilities, you're also sure you'll be one of those rare people who actually dies *from* doing taxes!

Taxes start out being difficult because you're being asked to take your slim profits and give some away — involuntarily. And you have to fill out time-consuming paperwork, knowing that any mistake could trigger an audit and/or a penalty. Add in that both federal and state revenue departments have created a system of complex instructions, deductions, loopholes, and payment schedules, and you have a recipe for one big headache.

This chapter doesn't try to substitute for those complex, difficult-to-digest documents from the Internal Revenue Service (IRS) or for your state and local revenue departments, but it does touch on the major tax liabilities that you may face — and perhaps even forget about — when taking care of running your bookshop.

A Little Bit on Every Sale: Retail Sales Tax

Unless you live in Delaware, Montana, New Hampshire, Oregon, or certain cities in Alaska, you pay sales tax — as a percentage of the selling price — on every product you ring up on your cash register.

After you collect the tax from your customers, you then report and pay it to your state government, using special forms that the state provides for you. Large tax liabilities usually mean more frequent filing; small tax liabilities usually result in paying less frequently, such as four times per year. Late fees and other penalties are usually imposed by the states.

Several states give you credit for the time you spend collecting sales tax on the state's behalf. This fee ranges from half a percent to five percent of the taxes you collect. Check with your state department of revenue to determine whether you're allowed to take this credit.

If your town borders a state with a lower income tax, you may be in competition with stores from across the border. To compete with these stores, determine what your customers really value:

- ✔ **Price?** Consider adjusting your retail prices to match your neighbors' non-tax totals.

- ✔ **Convenience?** Make certain your store is open when your customers want to shop. Use the Web, e-mail, and voice mail technology to allow your customers to search and order books anytime.

- ✔ **Selection?** Refine or expand your selection to your customers expectations (refer to Chapter 4).

- ✔ **Ambiance?** Improve the look and feel of your store in small ways that make a shopper feel better (refer to Chapter 7).

- ✔ **Customer service?** Make sure yours is worth the extra few cents on the dollar. You can find out what your customers want through surveys or informal conversations (see Chapters 3 and 9).

A little more on what's in your store: Inventory taxes

Before you file your federal taxes each year, you need to know the value of your inventory, which is why most bookshops conduct a full inventory once every year. This is a part of Schedule C, Part III (Cost of Goods Sold). You simply report your inventory at the beginning of the year, subtract purchases, shrinkage, and so on, and get a total that should equal the year's ending inventory.

Determine where the competition falls down by visiting their stores regularly. Invite staff suggestions and come up with a plan to meet or beat the stores across the border. After you implement your plan to be a worthy competitor, remember to aggressively promote your store and your services.

Taxes on Employees: Withholding

If you've been holding off hiring employees because you thought the Internal Revenue Service (IRS) paperwork was just too much to handle, you may be heartened by the fact that the IRS has begun a campaign to cut down on paperwork. Of course, this is still the IRS, a slow-moving branch of the federal government, so you're still inundated with paperwork — but the future does look a bit brighter for the federal income tax withholding form.

Knowing which taxes to withhold

As an employer, you pay two types of taxes for or on your employees:

✔ **Withheld Federal Income Tax,** including income tax, Social Security tax, and Medicare tax that you *withhold* (collect) from each employee's paycheck (although you pay a portion of this tax, too). To report this income, you use Form 941 each quarter and 945 annually. This tax includes tax on earned income (income tax) and taxes that pay for your employee's eventual use of Social Security and Medicare.

✔ **Employer's Annual Federal Unemployment (FUTA) Tax,** a separate, but equally important tax, that's paid roughly on the same schedule as withholding and requires Form 940.

Note that FUTA is paid by you and allows your employees to collect unemployment if they should become unemployed. You pay up to a certain amount on each employee; after you exceed that amount, your liability for FUTA stops. However, the more your employees receive unemployment benefits, the higher the rate you pay in FUTA. When you first begin paying FUTA, you pay at a fixed rate for one to three years before raising or lowering your rate, based on the frequency that your employees use the system.

Understanding how often to pay

Here's how these two federal taxes work: Periodically, you take the money you've withheld from your employees and pay it, as a lump sum, to the IRS in the following ways:

✔ If the total of your employees' income tax for the quarter (three months) is less than $2,500, you pay withholding taxes by the following dates:

- April 30 (for the period ending March 31)
- July 31 (for the period ending June 30)
- October 31 (for the period ending September 30)
- January 31 (for the period ending December 31)

If your FUTA is more than $100 per quarter, it's also due on the preceding dates. Otherwise, FUTA is due annually on January 31.

✔ If your payment to the IRS for a quarter will be $2,500 or more, and your total tax collected for employees for the preceding year (from July 1 to June 30) was $50,000 or less, you pay each month's taxes by the 15th day of the following month.

✔ If your payment to the IRS for a quarter will be $2,500 or more, and your total tax for the preceding year was more than $50,000, you pay on a semiweekly (every-other-week) schedule:

- • If your payday falls on a Wednesday, Thursday, or Friday, you deposit the taxes by the following Wednesday.

- • If your payday falls on a Saturday, Sunday, Monday, or Tuesday, you deposit taxes by the following Friday.

And, yes, that's the easy-to-understand system coming out of the new, streamlined, simplified IRS!

Making your deposits

You can make your federal tax deposits in three ways:

✔ Electronically, using the Electronic Federal Tax Payment System. If you use this system, you must initiate payment one day before it's due.

✔ At a bank or other financial institution, using Federal Tax Deposit (FTD) coupons (Form 8109), either in person or via mail.

✔ Mailing it directly to the IRS at the Federal Tax Deposit Processing Office.

When mailing deposits to your bank or to the IRS, your funds are supposed to be available to the IRS by your due date. However, if your envelope is postmarked two days before the due date, you're in like Flynn.

Filing forms

Each year, on January 31, you file Forms 945 (income, Social Security, and Medicare taxes) and 940 (FUTA). In addition, you file Form 941, the Employer's Quarterly Federal Tax Return on each of the following dates:

✔ April 30

✔ July 31

✔ October 31

✔ January 31

Deciding how much to withhold

To determine how much income tax to withhold, each employee completes Form W-4, and you use the information on that form to look up the payment due in the Tables for Percentage Method of Withholding. Although these tables are produced by the IRS, they're not that difficult to read. To find the tables and get a (concise?) 64-page document about these taxes, go to www.irs.gov and download Publication 15, Circular E, The Employer's Tax Guide.

IRS dates to keep in mind

Mark the following dates on your desk calendar to make sure that you're not socked with a penalty:

✔ **January 31:** File Form 940 (or 940EZ, which isn't that EZ), the Employer's Annual Federal Unemployment (FUTA) Tax Return. File Form 945, Annual Return of Withheld Federal Income Tax.

✔ **February 15:** Ask any employee who claimed an *exemption* (which means he or she didn't owe any taxes) on the previous year's Form W-4 to fill out a new W-4.

✔ **February 28:** File Copy A of all W-2s with the IRS. (If you file electronically, you have until March 31.)

✔ **April 30:** Deposit FUTA taxes for the first quarter. File Form 941, Employer's Quarterly Federal Tax Return. If tax liability for the quarter is under $2,500, pay Federal Income Tax payments.

✔ **July 31:** Deposit FUTA taxes for the second quarter. File Form 941, Employer's Quarterly Federal Tax Return. If tax liability for the quarter is under $2,500, pay Federal Income Tax payments.

✔ **October 31:** Deposit FUTA taxes for the third quarter. File Form 941, Employer's Quarterly Federal Tax Return. If tax liability for the quarter is under $2,500, pay Federal Income Tax payments.

✔ **December 1:** Request new W-2s from employees who need to change their withholding for the following year.

✔ **January 31:** Deposit FUTA taxes for the fourth and final quarter of the preceding year. File Form 941, Employer's Quarterly Federal Tax Return. If tax liability for the quarter is under $2,500, pay Federal Income Tax payments. Send Form W-2 to all employees.

Paying SUTA

In addition to the Federal Unemployment Tax (FUTA), many states also require that you pay State Unemployment Tax (SUTA). A general rule to follow is that if you pay at least $1,500 in wages in a quarter, you probably owe SUTA.

To determine your state's tax requirements for SUTA, contact your state department of revenue. An Internet search should do the trick.

Taxes on Profits: Corporate or Individual

Depending on how you've organized your bookstore, you pay taxes on profits in one of a variety of ways:

✔ **Sole proprietor:** As the sole proprietor (the simplest of all ways to organize a business), you and the bookstore are the same entity. (Note, however, that a sole proprietor can be only one person, not a married couple.) Although this set-up has potential legal ramifications (for example, if your store is sued, you're personally liable), store revenues are considered your own personal income and are taxed at your individual tax rate.

You can be a sole proprietor and still have a business name that's different from your personal name.

✔ **Partnership:** In a partnership, you share the business responsibilities with another person (often a spouse, sibling, or good friend). Each partner profits from the store, based on the terms of the partnership agreement, but each partner files a separate tax return and has that portion of the store's profits taxed as personal income.

A *general partner* usually manages the day-in/day-out functions of the bookstore, while a *limited partner* provides funding for the bookstore but little day-to-day input.

✔ **Corporation:** A corporation is a separate legal entity from its owners that provides numerous legal benefits but few tax benefits. Corporations are taxed twice: Once on corporate profits and a second time as shareholder's equity. In other words, the bookstore, as a corporation, files its own set of tax returns. You, as a full or part owner (shareholder) in the company, are taxed on company dividends paid to you. You're also taxed on whatever regular income the corporation pays you.

An *S corporation* (as opposed to a C corporation, the standard sort of corporation that's described in the preceding paragraph), is a more flexible version of a corporation that strongly resembles a partnership. Some states, however, don't offer this option. Check out *Small Business For Dummies,* 2nd Edition, by Eric Tyson and Jim Schell (Wiley Publishing, Inc.), for more information on corporations and other ways to organize your bookshop.

✔ Limited Liability Corporation (LLC): An LLC offers all the benefits of a corporation (legal protection) and those of a sole proprietorship or partnership (no double taxation). This is the most popular route for new small retail businesses in the United States.

The organization of a business may change over the years. You may begin your bookstore as a sole proprietor, for example, and later make the determination that changing to an S corporation makes sense for your growing company.

For any determinations that you make, enlist the help of an accountant or business advisor who's familiar with the particulars of your business. You also want to seek professional legal advice to create a partnership agreement or file the paperwork for any type of corporation.

Chapter 13

Using Financial Statements Effectively

*R*aise your hand if keeping the "business" books is, without a doubt, your least favorite part of life as a bookseller. If your hand's up, you're in good company. Financial documents are difficult to understand, time-consuming to create, and yield little of value on a day-to-day basis, right?

Managing your store's finances does take time and energy. But understanding your store's financial picture helps you run a tighter ship. By deftly utilizing the three major reports discussed in this chapter — operating statement, balance sheet, and cash-flow statement — you can keep your business out of trouble and use the information to help your business grow and thrive.

So, dust off your pocket protector and get out your calculator. This chapter takes you on a whirlwind tour of what you need to keep your business healthy.

Making a Statement about Operating Expenses

An *operating statement,* also known as a *profit-and-loss statement* or *P&L,* focuses on the profitability of your company over a set period of time: a month, a quarter (three months), or a year. In the end, a P&L shows the profit or loss of your business over whatever length of time you choose (for many booksellers, that period is quarterly, but newer, easy-to-use financial software makes a monthly P&L possible). You can then compare your current P&L to previous operating statements or to the bookselling industry as a whole, or you can focus on particular components of the P&L that can make your business more profitable.

In a nutshell, a P&L shows the following:

Sales revenue – expenses = profit (or loss)

Identifying the major components of a P&L

A P&L looks at five areas of your business:

✔ **Revenues over a specified amount of time:** *Revenue* simply means sales: what books and other products you sold during the month, quarter, or year.

✔ **Amount that the products you sold cost you to buy:** This measure is called *Cost of Goods Sold,* and it includes the following:

- The amount of your inventory at the beginning of the period (month, quarter, or year). In other words, what was on your bookstore shelves on the first day? Be sure to use the amount this inventory cost you (called *cost*), not the amount you charge your customers for it (called *list* or *retail*).

- Additional books and sidelines you purchased for resale during the period. Again, use cost. Add this amount to the starting inventory.

- Discounts taken for speedy payment for your inventory. This amount is subtracted from the two preceding amounts.

- Any returns back to publishers during this period. This amount is also subtracted.

- Whatever inventory you have on hand when the period ends (at the end of the month, quarter, or year). This amount is also subtracted.

What's left is the amount you actually paid for the inventory you sold during the set period of time.

When you subtract the cost of goods sold from your revenue, the amount left is called *Gross Profit.*

✔ **Expenses over that same specified amount of time:** Expenses include payroll (including your own salary), rent, phone, and other basic office expenses, bags for the cash-wrap area, industry publications, insurance, shipping, taxes (*not* including income taxes your business must pay to federal and state/local governments), and any other expenses you incur.

You subtract your expenses from your gross profit. The resulting amount is called *Operating Income* or *Operating Profit (*or *Loss).*

✔ **Other income and expenses during that time:** *Other income* includes interest earned while money sits in the bank and income from rental properties, for example. *Other expenses* include the interest paid on loans or store credit cards.

Note: You add your *other income* to and subtract your *other expenses* from the *operating income,* netting a figure known as *Net Income Before Tax.* If you don't have any income or expenses that fit this category of "other," operating income and net income before taxes are the same amount!

Do you wonder why Net Income Before Tax is even recorded? After all, you have to pay taxes, so the number you're most interested in is Net Income After Tax. Here's why you need this particular number: Because taxes can vary so much from one locale to another, by comparing your Net Income Before Tax to that of other bookshops around the country, you're taking out that variability that comes from different tax structures and truly comparing apples to apples.

✔ **Income taxes for that period:** This category includes money paid on your income (but not your payroll tax, sales tax collections, and so on).

You subtract your taxes from your operating expenses or net income before taxes, and you get the proverbial bottom line in this accounting business. That number — the mother of all financial figures — is called *Net Income After Tax,* also called *the bottom line.*

Using a P&L to improve your business

Table 13-1 shows a sample P&L for an independent bookstore. Note that the expenses listed under "Less: Expenses" are pretty standard fare for booksellers, and they tend to coincide with the business expense categories commonly accepted by the Internal Revenue Service (IRS).

Getting professional help

Chances are, you need professional help — with your finances, that is. Although you can fill out statements and other financial documents on your own (or with the help of a part-time bookkeeper), you still may want an accountant or other trusted business advisor to look at your books and advise you.

Some booksellers worry about sharing their financial information, but a second set of trained, objective eyes can see income or expense patterns that you may miss — and make recommendations for action before a problem materializes. You also can

expect any professional, whether an accountant or a business consultant who specializes in the bookstore business, to maintain the confidentiality of your numbers. Don't be afraid to ask a prospective advisor to review his or her confidentiality policies with you.

If you're working with a financial professional who isn't very knowledgeable about bookstores, be sure to prepare him or her before sharing your books. Explain the small *margins* (profits) in the bookselling biz, so that your professional can review your numbers without fainting.

Table 13-1 Archetype Bookshop's Operating Statement for Quarter Ending March 31, 20XX

	Dollars	Percent of Sales
Sales	150,000	100.00
Less: Cost of Good Sold	91,515	61.01
Gross Profit	58,485	38.99
Less: Expenses		
Payroll — owner's compensation	8,220	5.48
Payroll — employee compensation	18,285	12.19
Benefits	1,530	1.02
Occupancy (rent plus utilities)	12,525	8.35
Paid advertising	2,820	1.88
Phone	855	0.57
Professional services or consultation	945	0.63
Supplies	1,560	1.04
Depreciation	1,410	.94
Travel	525	0.35
Insurance (other than medical)	600	0.40
Credit card processing	1,380	.92
Dues and subscriptions	360	.24
Misc. Office/Postage	1,455	.97
Taxes (other than income tax)	900	0.60
Other operating expenses	1,830	1.22
Total Operating Expenses	55,200	36.80
Operating Income	3,285	2.19
Other income	165	.11
Other expenses	1,515	1.01
Net Income Before Tax	1,935	1.29
Income Taxes	536	0.36
Net Income After Tax	1,399	0.93

The biggies: Rent and payroll

The largest expense lines on most bookstore operating statements are Occupancy Costs and Payroll Expense. Even if you keep every other item on your P&L in line or below industry standards for a profitable bookstore, you can end up losing money if you're paying too much rent or carrying too large a payroll.

If your rent is on the high side (say, 9 or 10 percent of your sales), you need to keep your payroll (including your salary) lower than average (for example, 16 percent instead of 19 percent). If your store carries a large payroll (maybe you have two floors of selling space or a lot of outside events, for example), you need to keep your rent well under control.

Controlling rent and payroll aren't easy, but you do have some options. Ask your landlord to renegotiate your lease. Buy your building (the best guarantee against rent increases or a bad economy). Ask your staff to cut back their hours voluntarily (and keep their jobs, which is better than the alternative), which means that you'll have to spend more time working in the store yourself *(sweat equity).*

You can also offset high payroll, high occupancy costs, or any other expense by increasing your sales. Gather the brains of your bookstore together and see what you can do to create more sales without adding any more costs to your business.

After you fill in your own P&L each month, quarter, or year, what do you do? If you let your P&L sit in a thick binder and never look at it again, you've wasted your time — although that binder probably looks impressive. Instead of letting it gather dust, use your P&L as the helpful tool it can be:

✔ **Compare the revenue and expenses to the same period a year ago, paying careful attention to any changes in your expenses or income (revenue).** If revenue is down and/or expenses are up, think about what has changed: Are you still making good book-buying decisions (refer to Chapters 5 and 6), are your employees serving the needs of your customers, and are customers going elsewhere to purchase books? By comparing one period to the same period one year earlier, you notice early on whether your bookshop is on an upward or downward trend. (And, of course, if revenue is up and expenses are down, break out the champagne!)

Note that your most accurate comparison comes from dividing each expense by sales to come up with a percentage (refer to Table 13-1). You often have to spend more to make more, so as your revenue goes up, you can determine whether your expenses are going up an appropriate amount or too much.

✔ **Compare your percentages for costs of goods sold and expenses against that of other booksellers around the country.** ABA surveys independent bookstores around the country in a program known as ABACUS. If you haven't participated in the survey, consider doing so; after all, the more booksellers participate, the more representative the results will be. ABA makes the process easy (the survey takes about 45 minutes, once every year), and your financial information is protected because it's consolidated with the reports of other stores like yours, based on volume or region or other pertinent business factors. The goal of the ABACUS program is to provide booksellers with *financial benchmarks* (numbers to which you can compare your store). By checking your numbers against the measurements provided by ABACUS, you can evaluate how well your business is performing and identify areas where you need to improve. For more information, check out ABA's Web site at www. bookweb.org.

✔ **Investigate each line of the P&L one by one.** Two bookstores that reside in similar towns, with similar inventory and similar customers, may have very different Net Income Before Taxes. That's because the small decisions you make about expenses can add up quickly. If, for example, you can shave a few thousand dollars off your Cost of Goods Sold by paying the bills early and taking the additional discounts sometimes offered — plus find a way to save $500 on your phone bills by changing carriers, reduce your advertising budget by taking advantage of more free advertising (refer to Chapter 8) or e-mailing newsletters rather than mailing them (refer to Chapter 10), save on travel expenses by buying airline tickets one month ahead of time and staying in a hotel a mile from the convention or other event — you may find that your bottom line is vastly different from what it would have been otherwise.

Taking an inventory turn for the better

Inventory turnover (also called *inventory turns*) measures how efficiently your inventory (books, sidelines, and other products) generates revenue (that is, actual sales). Calculate inventory turns as follows:

Inventory turns
= total sales (at list price)
÷ inventory on hand (at list price)

Many booksellers aim for an average inventory turn of 3 per year. This doesn't mean that literally every book sells three copies per year, but rather that your shop's bestselling sections may turn at a rate of 5 or 6, and the slower moving sections may achieve a turn of only 2. If your inventory turn comes out at less than 3, you probably need to evaluate your stock. Are you ordering too many copies at a time? If so, take advantage of quick wholesaler turnaround and order fewer copies more frequently. Do you

have books that aren't selling at all? Then take advantage of your returns privileges. Depending on the size of your store and how many sidelines you sell, you may be able to turn your inventory more than 3 times per year.

Keep in mind that the higher your turnover, the more sales you're generating from your inventory, which means you have more cash to put in the bank, pay off debts, order more inventory, and so on. This improves your bottom line. At the same time, if you see a section with super-high turns (say 6, 8, or 10), you may be understocking that category: In other words, if you had more titles on hand, you'd probably sell more books from that section. And if you don't add some variety to a tiny, fast-moving section, you risk losing all the sales in that category when your loyal customers run out of books to read.

One of the best ways to improve your bottom line is to control expenses. An even better way is to increase your revenues (that is, sell more books). Just make sure that you increase sales in a way that doesn't produce so many more expenses that you end up with less profit in the end. So, if you sell 100 books at an event, but the event was costly and increased your expenses, you haven't become more profitable. To make your store more profitable, you want to increase your revenue and decrease or maintain your cost of goods sold and expenses at the same time.

✔ **Spend your Net Income After Tax wisely.** If your Net Income After Tax is $0 or a small amount, should you worry? After all, you've paid for your inventory, paid all of your employees' salaries and benefits (including your own), paid all of the expenses associated with maintaining a storefront, bought insurance for your company, paid taxes, and so on. What do you need more money for? Plenty. Use it as a rainy-day fund for the months, quarters, or years when revenues dip (as they usually do, from time to time). Use profits as a way to upgrade your store with new carpet, paint, displays, windows, and so on. Use it as a way to finance growth, whether that's a new location, a remodel, or an expanded section.

Striking a Balance with a Balance Sheet

Unlike a P&L, which gives financial information for a certain period of time, a balance sheet (sometimes called a *statement of financial purpose*) is a snapshot of your business the day the sheet is completed. This snapshot day is usually the last day of your P&L period (so, that means the last day of the month, quarter, or year).

If you've ever taken an accounting class, you've seen a balance sheet, which includes the following information:

✔ **Financial assets:** *Assets* include money you have ready, expect to receive, or can get from selling something you own. Consider whether you have any of the following assets, which are usually listed in order of *liquidity* (cash) within the next year: Those that are cash or the most like cash first, followed by other assets that could be turned into cash with some work.

- **Cash:** What's in your cash register or in the bank.

- **Accounts Receivable:** Amounts that customers owe you but haven't yet paid.

- **Inventory:** The books and other products you have for sale in your store (at cost).

Bookstores differ from other retailers in that inventory is considered a liquid asset because you can return unsold books to publishers or wholesalers. You may need to clue your accountant or your loan officer into this difference from the norm.

- **Other Current Assets:** Prepaid rent (rent that you've paid a month or two in advance but haven't yet used) and other similar expenses.

- **Noncurrent Assets (often called *Fixed Assets*):** Any assets that help you generate revenue beyond this year, like bookshelves, computers, your building (if you own it), and so on. These assets could be sold if needed, but because they tend to lose value with time *(depreciate),* these types of assets are listed separately from the four preceding current assets, which could easily be sold or refunded.

Keep in mind that the assets you list have to be financial in nature. Unfortunately, this means that your "stunning intellect" or "friendship with Stephen King" doesn't appear in the financial assets column.

✓ **Financial liabilities and Owner's Equity:** Liabilities and owner's equity show how the assets were paid for or financed or, said another way, they show the sources for the funds used to acquire the assets. *Liabilities* are those creditors that you'll pay back at a later date, while *Owner's Equity* (sometimes called *net worth*) refers to cash that you or other investors put into the company to pay for some of the assets. Liabilities fall in to the following categories:

- **Accounts Payable:** What you owe to creditors for your inventory, supplies, or anything else paid for with credit that you expect to pay in the next 12 months.

- **Other Current Liabilities:** Other liabilities include *accrued expenses* (utilities used but not yet paid for, hours that your employees worked but that you haven't paid, and so on) and *deferred revenue* (items that customers have paid for but not yet received, which may happen with large orders or orders placed on your Web site). All of these liabilities are due and payable in the next 12 months.

- **Long-Term Liabilities:** Payments due on loans beyond 12 months, including a mortgage on your store. Note that the mortgage due *this year* is a current liability, whereas the amount due next year, and the next, and the next, is a long-term liability.

Because a balance sheet has to, appropriately enough, *balance*, the Owner's Equity = Assets – Liabilities. Owner's Equity may be put back into the business (called *retained earnings*) or distributed in the form of dividends to stockholders (if you operate as a corporation) or to you (as the owner).

A balance sheet (see a sample in Table 13-2), helps you to make sure that your level of debt isn't too high and that you have sufficient funds to pay off your debt along the timeline you've been given.

Table 13-2 Archetype Bookshop's Balance Sheet on March 31, 20XX

	Dollars	Percent of Total
ASSETS		
Current Assets:		
Cash	19,084	14.28
Accounts Receivable	1,740	1.30
Inventory	101,000	75.59
Other Current Assets	1,661	1.24
Total Current Assets	123,485	92.42
Fixed Assets	10,132	7.58
Total Assets	133,617	100.00
LIABILITIES AND OWNER'S EQUITY		
Current Liabilities:		
Accounts Payable	28,874	21.61
Other Current Liabilities	4,848	3.63
Long-Term Liabilities	12,724	9.52
Total Liabilities	46,446	34.76
Owner's Equity (Net Worth)	87,171	65.24
Total Liabilities and Owner's Equity	133,617	100.00

The point of no return (on investment)

Return on investment (ROI) is a measure of how efficiently you're earning a profit on your investment in your bookshop. With all likelihood, you didn't get into the bookselling biz to make a killer return on your original investment. However, if you ever apply for a loan or try to attract investors to expand your business, you'll need to understand what this means. To figure the return on your investment, use the following formula:

ROI = Net Income Before Tax (from P&L) ÷ Owner's Equity (from balance sheet) × 100

Generally, the higher the ROI, the better, because you're getting a higher return on a smaller amount of money, which is a good thing. Compare this number to interest rates you could earn at the bank or returns in the stock market today. Of course, you expect your ROI to be higher than what you could earn at the bank because you've taken on far more risk.

Going with the Flow: Cash-Flow Projections

A *cash-flow projection* (or *cash-flow statement*) shows cash flowing into and out of your bookstore. By preparing a cash-flow statement, you can estimate when, from where, and how much cash will flow into your store and compare that to when and how much cash needs to flow out.

A cash-flow projection can be of critical importance to your store because it tells you whether you'll have enough cash to cover your expenses when they're due. Without a cash-flow projection, you may show a profit at the end of the year, but also may have had periods during which you ran out of cash and were unable to

- ✔ Make payroll.
- ✔ Pay the rent or mortgage.
- ✔ Make timely payments to wholesalers and publishers.

Not being able to pay your employees, your landlord (or your mortgage company), and/or your sources of inventory substantially weakens your business. These key players in your business have to trust that you'll pay your bills on time. Creating a cash-flow projection worksheet and entering your actual figures against your projections helps you make important decisions when sales fall short of expectations; for example, you can adjust staffing, changing buying patterns, and/or send back returns to offset publisher payables.

In an interest-bearing account that's separate from your checking account, consider keeping enough cash on hand to pay your projected bills for two or three months. If this isn't possible, try to establish a line of credit at your bank that you can tap if you ever see your cash-flow projection dipping into negative numbers.

To project your cash flow, follow these steps:

1. **Start with a projection of your store's income.**

   If you've been in business for a year or longer, hunt down your sales figures for this day of the week one year ago. (If you simply match up the dates, you may end up comparing Friday sales to Saturday sales, for example, which may not be very accurate.) You can also project figures for a week or a month, rather than estimating day-by-day. Oddly enough, many book-sellers find that daily cash flow is easier to project, because they track sales on a daily basis. In Table 13-3 at the end of the chapter, you see a daily projection for two weeks time. You can adapt this table in whatever way works best for your store.

   Even if you haven't been in business for a year, you can still use historical data. If you made $500 last Tuesday, and tomorrow is another Tuesday, you can estimate that you'll make at least $500 tomorrow — probably even more, because you're in the growth years of your business. Of course, if last Tuesday was the day before Christmas or the first day of a week-long festival attended by tens of thousands of tourists, or the release date of the latest Harry Potter book, last week's numbers may not jibe with what's going to happen tomorrow. When projecting sales figures, always use common sense so that you get the best possible estimate!

2. **Multiply that number by somewhere between 90 and 115 percent.**

In a difficult economy or a down period for book sales, be conservative. Project at the low end — for example, that you'll make 90 percent of what you made on the same day (or week or half-month) last year — because that way, you're counting on getting less money that you probably will, and this makes you feel more secure that your expenses will be covered. If your store is on the upswing and you have every reason to believe that this year's sales will be higher than last year's, go with the high end, say 105 to 115 percent of last-year's income. The risk in estimating too high, of course, is that you may believe your expenses will be covered by your high sales, and if those sales don't pan out, you may be short of cash for your expenses.

3. **Determine when you'll be getting that money you've projected in sales.**

   This sounds like a no-brainer, right? Well, it's really not. If, for example, 50 percent of your income is in the form of checks or debit cards, 40 percent of your income tends to come from credit cards, and the rest comes from cash, consider the following:

   - 10 percent of your money will be in your hands when you close (that's from the cash you received)

   - 50 percent will be in your hands within two business days (that's from the checks and debit cards)

   - 40 percent will be in your hands in two to four business days (those are the credit card payments)

   If you want to make this process even simpler, don't break your income down this accurately. Simply expect that you'll receive all of the income in four days and proceed with your projections.

4. **Enter this information on a spreadsheet, showing when each percentage of your projected income will be deposited.**

   Keep the system simple: Enter the date at which you'll receive cash from tomorrow's sales and the amount you'll likely get, so that you know exactly when you'll have cash on hand to pay your bills.

   Microsoft Excel is extremely useful for keeping track of this sort of data, and it's not that difficult to master.

Check out *Excel For Dummies* by Greg Harvey (Wiley Publishing, Inc.) if you run into trouble.

One of the many advantages to using a computer spreadsheet program is that you can use this year's actual numbers as the basis for next year's projections. You can even ask Excel to apply a percentage to those numbers (supposing a happy 110% of this year's sales, for example) to create the projections for next year.

5. **In that same spreadsheet, spell out the checks you know you have to write.**

   Include the following information:

   - Payee

   - Amount

   - What for

   - When it's due or when the payment should be sent

6. **As soon as you know your actual sales and your real bills, input those numbers into the your worksheet, too.**

   Based on what you see, you can determine whether you have enough money to pay the bills (or in the dream situation, you need to increase staffing to handle higher-than-expected sales).

Exactly how you decide to compare your projections with your actual numbers depends on your level of experience with spreadsheet software, the accuracy you expect from your cash-flow projections, and the simplicity you're looking for in your system.

Table 13-3 gives you an example of a daily cash-flow analysis that's done in checkbook format, so that it gives a running projected balance. Note that the projections here are conservative — don't be afraid to make yours significantly higher if that makes sense for your business. This cash-flow projection also assumes that all sales revenue will be processed by the bank within four business days, which makes the analysis simpler than estimating exactly when credit cards and checks will clear the bank. Although the balance drops precipitously after several bills come due, the bookshop owner still has every confidence that those bills can be paid. The next few weeks of sales will begin to raise the balance again.

Table 13-3   Archetype Bookshop's Daily Cash-Flow Projection

Date Received or Send Date	Type of Income or Expense	Sales Last Year	Projected Sales at 95%	Projected Expense	Projected Cash Balance	Actual Sales This Year	Actual Expenses This Year	Actual Cash Position
				Beginning Balance:	$17,350.00		Beginning Balance:	$17,350.00
Friday, July 20	7/16 sales	$ 1,570.00	$ 1,491.50	$ -	$ 18,841.50	$ 1,617.10	$ -	$18,967.10
Monday, July 23	7/17 sales	$ 1,600.00	$ 1,520.00	$ -	$ 20,361.50	$ 1,648.00	$ -	$20,615.10
Tuesday, July 24	7/18 sales	$ 1,450.00	$ 1,377.50	$ -	$ 21,739.00	$ 1,493.50	$ -	$22,108.60
Wednesday, July 25	7/19 sales	$ 2,350.00	$ 2,232.50	$ -	$ 23,971.50	$ 1,997.50	$ -	$24,106.10
Thursday, July 26	7/20 sales	$ 2,666.00	$ 2,532.70	$ -	$ 26,504.20	$ 2,692.66	$ -	$26,798.76
Friday, July 27	Payroll	$ -	$ -	$ 4,417.00	$ 22,087.20	$ -	$ 5,079.55	$21,719.21
Friday, July 27	Favorite Wholesalers	$ -	$ -	$ 5,780.00	$ 16,307.20	$ -	$ 6,647.00	$15,072.21
Friday, July 27	Favorite Publishers	$ -	$ -	$ 6,383.00	$ 9,924.20	$ -	$ 7,340.45	$7,731.76
Friday, July 27	United Phone Co.	$ -	$ -	$ 307.00	$ 9,617.20	$ -	$ 353.05	$7,378.71
Friday, July 27	7/21 sales	$ 3,001.00	$ 2,850.95	$ -	$ 12,468.15	$ 2,970.99	$ -	$10,349.70
Friday, July 27	7/22 sales	$ 1,780.00	$ 1,691.00	$ -	$ 14,159.15	$ 2,136.00	$ -	$12,485.70
Monday, July 29	7/23 sales	$ 1,201.00	$ 475.00	$ -	$ 14,634.15	$ 546.25	$ -	$13,031.95
Tuesday, July 30	7/24 sales	$ 1,305.00	$ 1,239.75	$ -	$ 15,873.90	$ 1,859.63	$ -	$14,891.58
Wednesday, July 31	7/25 sales	$ 1,650.00	$ 1,567.50	$ -	$ 17,441.40	$ 1,489.13	$ -	$16,380.70
Thursday, August 1	Kindly Landlord, Inc.	$ -	$ -	$ 4,871.00	$ 12,570.40	$ -	$ 4,871.00	$11,509.70
Thursday, August 1	Hometown News & Times	$ -	$ -	$ 680.00	$ 11,890.40	$ -	$ 680.00	$10,829.70
Thursday, August 1	Publisher's Periodicals	$ -	$ -	$ 85.00	$ 11,805.40	$ -	$ 85.00	$10,744.70
Thursday, August 1	Electric and Water Co.	$ -	$ -	$ 635.00	$ 11,170.40	$ -	$ 635.00	$10,109.70
Thursday, August 1	7/26 sales	$ 2,300.00	$ 2,185.00	$ -	$ 13,355.40	$ 2,461.00	$ -	$12,570.70
Friday, August 2	7/27 sales	$ 2,788.00	$ 2,648.60	$ -	$ 16,004.00	$ 2,983.16	$ -	$15,553.86

Part V
The Part of Tens

The 5th Wave   By Rich Tennant

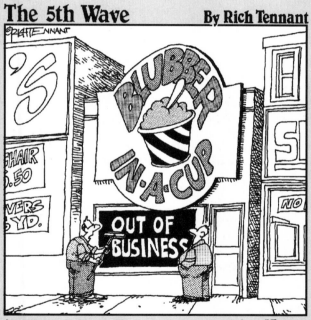

"It's hard to figure. The concept was a big hit in Nome."

In this part . . .

Y ou find four quick chapters, and each one gives you ten tips and tidbits of information. Here, you find ten great ways to get customers in your door, ten timely tips for lowering costs, ten ideas for motivating employees, and ten reasons why bookselling is the best job in the world.

Chapter 14

Ten Ways to Get More Customers through the Door

*T*he best way to generate more revenue is to get customers in the door. Even if they don't buy the first time, if they have a great experience, they'll be back and will eventually become steady customers.

Getting Involved in the Community

What sets your store apart from corporate superstores and mass merchandisers is that yours is a community bookstore (refer to Chapter 8). Involve yourself deeply in your community: Throw your doors open to whomever needs your store and stop thinking about profit for the moment.

✔ Is a local organization asking you for a door prize or raffle item? Give a generous store gift certificate, which some lucky customer will come to the store to redeem.

✔ Do groups want to meet at your store? Let them — this approach gets people in the door and makes them appreciate what you're doing for them.

✔ Does a school or other not-for-profit want you to sell books at an event they're staging and give them a portion of the profits? Do it. You may not make a bundle of money, but people will remember that you helped make the event happen. You're marketing the store at the same time that you're selling books.

✔ Does a local author want to stage an event at your store, and you're not sure whether customers are looking for this type of event? Organize the event anyway and go all out: Send out e-mail invitations, hang a welcome banner for the author, and provide refreshments. You'll reap the benefits of goodwill from the author and his or her family and friends.

✔ Is the local library asking you to partner up for an event? Take advantage of this opportunity to put your store's name in front of booklovers in your community.

Holding Socially Meaningful Events

Unlike other retail businesses that tend to stay socially neutral, bookstores are often expected to be a gathering place for social views and values that may not be politically popular. Booksellers often feel a deep conviction that books are an important part of the culture and shouldn't be muzzled, especially when writers and poets are speaking in protest or dissent and plan events that support this conviction.

Northshire Bookstore in Manchester, Vermont, recently seized on an opportunity to host such an event. After a White House reading by several poets whose views ran contrary to political sentiment was cancelled, Northshire invited the poets to read at the bookstore, instead. *The New York Times* picked up on the story and as a result, customers came through the doors in droves.

Offering a Unique Experience

Want to get customers in the door? Be a special store and offer products, experiences, and relationships they can't get anywhere else. Respond not just to national trends and ideas but to local ones, too. Be sure you're serving your unique customer base in a unique way: A bookstore in Duluth should be a different experience for customers than one in Miami or Seattle.

Opening Your Door (s)

Literally — open your door! In fair weather, keep your door open every day as a means of inviting customers into your store.

You also want to extend your store to the out-of-doors as much as possible. Put out a sale cart (under-your awning, if you have one) or place a couple of café tables outside your shop for customers to sit and read or visit with friends. Even if your shop doesn't include a coffee shop or café, set up a small area with free coffee or lemonade for customers to take outside and enjoy.

Giving Your Store a Face-Lift

If customers are flocking to a new corporate superstore, consider sprucing up a bit to make your shop seem new, too. Can the store use new paint, new artwork on the walls, or new carpeting? Do the shelves need dusting and have your signs and banners taken a beating? Do your displays change regularly enough to draw new customers? Do what you can afford to make your store seem shiny and new.

Maintaining a Web Site

A Web site serves as a fantastic tool for bringing in new and existing customers. Whether a customer finds you as a result of an Internet search or you've advertised your site so well that customers log on to see what you have to offer, a Web site is just as powerful and important to your store as your phone line is.

Believe it or not, some customers prefer looking at books online to browsing your store. When you offer a full-service Web site that competes with other Internet bookstores, you're extending your store into customers' offices, kitchens, and dens. If you still want to get those customers to come into your store, give them a reason to pick up the books they've ordered — like a free cup of really good coffee when they do.

Giving Customers an Incentive

Market your store to your local area with a tease, incentive, or discount. You don't have to offer 20 percent off everything in the store; instead, target one book, one category of books (such as baseball books), or one type of customer (teachers, for example) that receives a discount, and advertise the incentive on store signs, flyers, and ads. If you target one book and picture it in an ad or on banners, apply for co-op money (refer to Chapter 5) for that promotion.

Serving Your Customers

When customers come into your store for the first time, you have an opportunity to evoke one of two kinds of responses: a great experience that they want to repeat or a poor experience that they want to avoid in the future.

Are you open when your customers want to shop? Make sure your store hours match the needs of your customers (and this usually means staying open a little later than you may like). When you're closed, make sure your customers still can reach you — whether through a user-friendly voice-mail system or via your 24/7 Web site.

Cultivating Word of Mouth

When you provide value and great service to your customers, they tell others about your store. Always be mindful of opportunities to develop new customers through your existing ones.

Putting Yourself in Your Customer's Shoes

When you want to increase traffic in your bookshop, put yourself into your customer's shoes: Approach your store as if you were the customer. Think about whether the display in the window or event in your store would draw you in. What will the experience be like after the customer walks in? Will the person be back? Then try to address the stumbling blocks.

Chapter 15

Ten Ideas for Lowering Costs

*I*f your profits are low (refer to Chapter 13), you can improve them in two ways: by raising revenues and lowering expenses. To find out how to increase revenues (by getting customers in the door), refer to Chapter 14. In this chapter, you discover a variety of ways to reduce your costs.

Partnering Up

If advertising an event is too expensive, partner with an organization in your community that has a vested interest in what you're trying to do, and it'll help you make the event a big splash:

✔ Join with the media (newspaper, NPR station, AM stations) and make your event their event so that they advertise it for free. Be sure to include the media outlet's name on everything that advertises the event and ask someone from the newspaper or radio station to kick off the event as a guest speaker.

✔ Find for-profit and/or not-for-profit groups that share a common interest with the event. For example, team up with the AMA when a doctor comes in to talk about cholesterol levels. For a hiking book, team up with a local hiking group that helps with advertising and/or refreshments.

Taking Advantage of Co-op Money

Don't let any co-op dollars (refer to Chapter 5) go unused. Pay attention to the dollars that are available and create a system to use and collect co-op. You may be able to fund all or almost all of your events, newsletters, and Internet site fees by using co-op money.

E-mailing Your Newsletters and Event Invitations

Even if you're paying only $700 or $800 to send out each newsletter or catalog, compared to the e-mailed newsletter's price of zero/zilch/nada, you can save a bundle.

The same goes for event postcards. Printing and mailing the postcards may be an expense you can eliminate by developing an e-mail mailing list (refer to Chapter 10) and sending reminders a few days before each event.

Setting Up a Sale Rack Special

Although you can almost always return books for a credit from publishers (refer to Chapter 6), you can save on the return freight, improve your cash flow, and reduce paperwork by selling overstocks to customers at your wholesale cost instead of returning the books to publishers.

In order to sell overstocks successfully, rotate your stock. When you pull a book for a return, put it on sale for one or two weeks at most and keep adding new books every few days. If a book doesn't sell in that week or two, return it just as you would have otherwise (and keep your sale area fresh at the same time). Don't put remainders or bestsellers on the cart, or you'll train customers to wait for sales for those types of books. By rotating the stock frequently, you get customers to come by more often to check for sale items.

Analyzing Your Spending

Always monitor your expenses, keeping careful track of your profit-and-loss statement (P&L — refer to Chapter 13). Pay attention to where you're spending the most money and work to reduce those costs. Look especially carefully at rent and payroll (the two largest operating expenses). Don't spend too much time finding out how to reduce the price of your bookmarks from 5.5¢ to 4.5¢, unless that reduction will net you thousands per year in savings. Remember that your time is money, too: Concentrate on the biggies.

Compare your spending to other bookshops of your size through ABA's ABACUS program. The data is available through ABA and offers you a chance to see whether your expenses are higher than or in line with that of other stores. Refer to Chapter 13 for more.

Buying Your Building

If at all possible, buy the building you occupy. You'll be the best landlord you ever had — and depending on your location, you may be able to rent space to other merchants, too. Owning your building offers you financial flexibility in the short term and gives you long-term security in the form of a tangible asset that's bound to appreciate.

Controlling Your Inventory

Keep on the shelf only what you know you can put into customers' hands and sell. If a book doesn't sell in a season, return it before the next season.

Keep careful track of your inventory, ordering cautiously across the board. If you skimp on titles that are selling well or dramatically cut your inventory, you could end up selling from an empty cart. Rather than reducing the number of books you sell, try to get a better discount on the ones you do order. Look for deals and pay your bills early to get an additional small discount.

Keeping Track of Shipping Costs

Keep track of shipping on books that come in and on those that are returned. Some publishers do charge too much for shipping, so track it: Weigh packages and bring over-charges to the publishers' attention. When you place your frontlist orders, write or type on your purchase order "One shipment — no backorder — we will not pay for multiple shipments of this order." Because a purchase order is a contract, this language keeps publishers from sending multiple shipments, which dramatically increase shipping charges.

Conducting a Shift Analysis

A *shift analysis* looks at how many customers visit your store during various periods of the day and compares that figure to the number of booksellers you need on the floor to serve those customers. Your point-of-sales (POS) computer is probably already monitoring your transactions. Compare the number of sales per hour to the number of employees you have on hand. If you find you're overstaffed at slow times or understaffed when you're busiest, adjust your employee schedule accordingly.

Make sure that your employee schedule is driven by the needs of your customers, not by which employees need what hours each week. Cut back on hours, as needed, so that your staffing matches your anticipated sales.

Making Sure Your Community Services Serve You, Too

Being an important part of your community is critical to the success of your bookstore. But if you go out of business on giveaways, you won't be able to serve your community at all. Be as generous as you can with your space, your time, and your services, but be sure you can afford to provide all of the community services you're offering.

Chapter 16

Ten Ways to Motivate Employees

In This Chapter

▶ Finding ways to attract and retain employees

▶ Helping employees feel like an important part of your store

▶ Catching employees doing good work

*B*ookstore employees don't always make the best wages, especially taking into account their intelligence and skills. This chapter helps you find other ways to motivate your employees, who are on the front lines with customers every day.

Helping Your Employees Share Your Mission

Be open with employees about the mission of the store, being clear and consistent about what you're trying to accomplish. Your store should be an extension of your values, and employees don't always know what those are until you tell them.

Trusting Your Employees

Trust your employees, in spite of the few bad seeds who make you want to micromanage. Give them a key to the store, have them track their own hours (instead of using a time clock), and let them do some wholesale ordering for books they're passionate about and have a vested interested in handselling.

Empowering Employees to Help Customers

Give your employees the power to make decisions. Create a culture in which employees know that they can't make a wrong decision if they're making customers happy. You don't want employees who wait for you to reach a decision, because by that time the customer has become impatient or has already left. You can always talk about the decision later, but don't make your employees wait for your permission to fully serve a customer.

Matching Employees with Their Interests

Keep employees happy by giving them interesting projects to work on. Find out what categories, events, or tasks within the store (such as producing window displays) match their interests and let them run with it!

Offering a Generous Discount

Give a generous book discount, allowing employees to buy at cost. This practice encourages employees to read, makes them glad to be working at your bookshop, and doesn't cost you extra money.

Keep in mind that even purchasing books at cost may be a little expensive for your employees. Allow new books to be borrowed (without the dust jackets), as long as they're returned in pristine condition.

Sharing Publishers' Perks

If you receive freebies (tote bags, T-shirts, and other knick-knacks) from publishers or — better yet — you're able to get advance copies or galleys of frontlist titles, share these with your employees. Distribute them randomly or keep in mind which employees like which types of advance copies or give-aways, but try never to keep these perks to yourself.

In addition, when an author comes to visit, make sure that every employee has a chance to meet him or her individually. Meeting authors may have begun to seem mundane to you, but it's probably still a treat for most of your employees.

Sending Employees to Trade Shows

Send as many employees as you can to regional trade shows (splitting, for example, half of your staff between the two days of the show) or even to BEA when it's close by. Nothing makes an employee feel like part of the team more than going to trade shows, conferences, or any "business trip."

Arming Employees with Information

Your employees need to know what's going on in the publishing world, the news media, and your community. Arm them with information at daily or twice-daily meetings in which you discuss the hot new titles, upcoming events, and so on. The more knowledgeable your employees are, the more knowledge they can impart to customers.

Hold *category chats* once a month — after-work sessions in which employees are paid and food and beverages are served. As a group, you discuss what's hot, what's not, how the section is organized, important backlist items, and so on.

Giving Immediate Feedback

Employees want respect and validation for their contributions as much as they want money. Catch them doing good things and give them lots of praise. Buy gift certificates (in bulk) from local restaurants, the movie theaters, and so on, and give them out randomly when an employee has a great interaction with a customer, puts together a terrific display, or stays late to help out.

Paying as Well as Possible

Ultimately, money can be a great motivator: When you pay someone well, they give something special in return. One great way to pay well without stressing your budget is to offer bonuses tied to profitability. Doing so encourages employees to keep costs down and send revenues higher.

Chapter 17

Ten Reasons Why Bookselling Is the Best Job Ever

In This Chapter

▶ Remembering why you choose this profession

▶ Looking at what booksellers accomplish

*B*ookselling is about great products and great people. This chapter tells you why bookselling beats every other profession, hands-down.

Surrounding Yourself with Books

Bookselling is one of the few professions in which you can surround yourself with books. You probably can't imagine selling anything else, because you love the feel of a new book in your hand, you breathe in the smell of it, and you thrill at discovering a new author or great new title. In the course of your work, you get to order great books, read many of them, and share what you've read with others: Not a bad day's work.

Surrounding Yourself with Booklovers

As a bookseller, you get to live your life — at least your work-life — surrounded by booklovers. From authors to publishers to customers, you spend your days with people who believe in the culture of books.

Working an Interesting Day with a Variety of Tasks

One of the best aspects of bookselling is that your day is incredibly diverse and stimulating. Whether you're ordering inventory, helping a customer find an obscure book, answering a zillion questions, coordinating author events, running your cash-flow projections, or donating books or gift certificates to a local organization (and that's just your morning!), you get to do such a variety of tasks that you never get bored.

Developing a Relationship with Customers

Many customers come to your store because they want your personal advice. A book requires a much greater investment of time than a movie does, and customers want to make sure that investment is a wise one. You and your booksellers have a chance to make that investment pay off handsomely, so that customers come back time and time again for more of your knowledge and expertise.

Not every customer wants to have this type of relationship. The customers who don't come in for your advice are just as appreciative of your store as are other customers; they simply want to have a different type of relationship with you. This goes for your Internet customers, too (refer to Chapter 10).

Being a Part of the Larger Bookselling Community

Being a bookseller means becoming a colleague of — and perhaps even a mentor to — other booksellers around the country. Through ABA and the regional bookselling associations (refer to Chapter 1), you get to interact with some of the most enthusiastic, knowledgeable, and passionate entrepreneurs in the world.

Feeding People's Passions

A book exists for everyone — and you're often able to link customers with obscure books that exactly meet their needs. Whether customers' requests are deeply moving or ridiculous, you get to feed people's passion through the books you can find, order, and put into their hands.

Becoming a Cultural Meeting Place

Your store is likely a cultural meeting place that encourages serious discussion within book clubs, at Q&A sessions with authors, among customers who meet at the store, and in a variety of other ways.

You may also participate in a number of important social movements, from organizing protest marches to bringing together writers who offer unique voices to hanging contemporary artwork in your store to bringing in bands or the ballet for short programs. Your bookshop is *the* place in the community where free-thinking abounds.

Spreading Information to the Smallest Towns

Without books, small towns run the risk of being isolated from the ideas floating around the rest of the country — and world. Although television goes a long way toward connecting people, the three major networks and the various cable stations can't offer anywhere near the diversity of opinions that the thousands of books published every year can. Even in a small town, you can special order any book for customers, so that you get to disseminate the information that can help to keep them broad-minded, global thinkers.

Watching Kids Get Lost in Books

Watching a child develop a relationship with books is, in and of itself, worth the long hours and low margins. Books for kids come alive in such a different way than movies or TV cartoons do: Children lose themselves in the books and in their imaginations. The books they love become a part of their development and personalities.

Changing Customers' Lives

Being a bookseller is deeply satisfying because, at the end of the day, you know you've made a difference in people's lives. All the hard work becomes worthwhile on the days you make a customer laugh, help a customer gain information about a frightening illness, or put a book into a child's hands.

You have the potential to lead change in society and in the individuals who come in the door. Books are vehicles for change; books promote ideas, discussion, and debate. Books — even those that aren't bestsellers — can be extraordinarily influential.

Index